AN OFFER
They Can't Refuse

14 TOOLS TO CREATE
BETTER OFFERS
FOR NETWORK MARKETING

KEITH & TOM "BIG AL" SCHREITER

An Offer They Can't Refuse

© 2023 by Keith & Tom "Big Al" Schreiter

Published by Fortune Network Publishing

P.O. Box 890084

Houston, TX 77289 USA

+1 (281) 280-9800

BigAlBooks.com

info@BigAlBooks.com

Print ISBN: 978-1-956171-15-0

Ebook ISBN: 978-1-956171-16-7

CONTENTS

PREFACE

My network marketing friend calls me. We hadn't talked in over 20 years. I guess it is hard to keep up with everyone.

The conversation drags on.

Finally, after 30 minutes, my friend makes an offer for me to join his latest venture.

Groan.

Of course, the polite answer from me is "no", but this left me thinking.

He wasted 30 minutes of his time before he got to his offer.

I wasted 30 minutes of my time waiting for him to get to the point of this call.

That is 60 minutes of time we will never get back.

What if we had spent that time more productively such as discussing donuts? Or pizza? Or Mexican food?

Why is it important for us to create great offers?

Imagine this situation.

What if our new team members don't have great persuasion skills yet? That's normal. They just started.

But ... we provide our new team members with an outstanding offer that compels prospects to say, "Yes!" ... with no persuasion skills necessary! How great would that be?

Our new team members could get initial success while learning the basic skills of communication and persuasion for their business. All they need to do is to present an outstanding offer.

Prospects have choices. They hear offers every day. Most ordinary offers sound like this, "Give me money and I will give you my stuff so I can make a commission."

Ugh!

With this kind of competition, it won't be hard for us to shine.

So picture this.

Our prospects go about their lives and see two offers.

Offer #1 is ... okay.

Offer #2 is better.

Which offer will our prospects choose?

Let's make the better offer.

"P-S-S-S-T! HEY! YOU! YES, YOU!"

April 11, 2020

Local supermarket: Mexican food aisle 4

"P-s-s-s-t! Hey! You! Yes, you!"

A sketchy dude was trying to whisper in my ear. Cringe!

Now that is uncomfortable. Bad breath too.

He continued, "Shhh. Listen. I got a toilet paper connection. How many do you want?"

Well, the shelves were empty. Coronavirus in full swing. And this weird guy had a secret connection. My heart skipped a beat.

So I whispered back, "I'll take ten rolls."

He seemed offended. "Only ten rolls? You're gonna need more than that. You're standing here in the Mexican food aisle."

"Okay, I'll take 25 rolls of toilet paper. No problem. How much?"

"$10 a roll. I have the good stuff, not some single ply garbage." He seemed confident.

"Uh, that's kind of expensive, but ... no choice I guess. Where can we make the exchange?"

"I'll meet you in the parking lot in 5 minutes. Look for an unmarked black van. And bring small, unmarked bills."

Wait a minute!

This sketchy dude didn't build rapport. In fact, he could be a great example of anti-rapport!

The facts, features, and benefits were missing. He didn't even have a company video!

Hmmm, no word pictures either.

How about magic words?

No. They were missing too.

Great persuasion techniques?

No. He didn't even ask for the sale.

Just some sketchy dude trying to sell me overpriced toilet paper.

The lesson?

Rapport, ice breakers, and high-level persuasion skills are great ... but a powerful offer can sell itself.

Oh.

Ding!

Lightbulb moment.

Aha!

Our new team members have no skills when they start.

But ... but ... what if ... we did this?

What if we gave our new team members an incredible offer that almost sold itself? They could have some instant success while learning the skills of network marketing.

Ding!

And that is how we can give our new team members the best start ever!

All we need to do is provide them with a quick, simple, irresistible offer that prospects will think, "Hey! That sounds pretty good. That is better than what I have now."

And then?

Our new team members can take the volunteers.

The science and skills of making great offers

- How would it feel to have irresistible offers?
- How about an offer that prospects couldn't refuse?
- What if our offer was so clear that our prospects understood it instantly?
- What makes great offers?
- How can we make our offers unique so prospects won't shop around?
- When is the best time to take "risk" out of our offers?
- Can we personalize our offers in line with our prospects' internal programs?
- What if we could change an offer that would double our income?
- Where can we ...

Okay, we got the idea.

One good offer will change our career

Good news! We can learn the science and skills of making great offers.

Ask ourselves this question, "If we made great offers, instead of ordinary offers, would that make our business grow faster?"

Of course.

So how long do we want to wait?

How much longer do we want to stay at the same bonus check level?

Let's make great offers now that will change our network marketing career forever.

What are we waiting for?

Let's turn the page and get started.

"OH NO! I WOULD NEVER MAKE A SALES OFFER!"

Sure. Go ahead and believe that, but what is the reality?

We make offers every day to people who think like we do, want what we do, and value what we do. It's what humans do. We are social. We make offers to each other when we talk. It's how we interact and get along. Oh.

Oh yes, we are offer-making machines.

Ready to see some offers?

- "Do you wanna come with me to the donut shop?"
- "Will you pick up my children for me in return for my unending gratitude?"
- "If I bring pizza to your door, will you give me money?"
- "I will mow your lawn if you let me use your pool."
- "If you drive me to the airport, I'll pay for your gas."
- "I'll scratch your back if you scratch mine."
- "If you cook, I'll do the dishes."
- "Eat this snack and you won't feel hungry."
- "If you give me a raise, I won't quit this job."
- "If I give you a raise, will you stay on your job?"

- "If you work overtime on Saturday, you can have Monday off."
- "If you go out with me Friday night, I promise you will have a great time."

We make offers almost every time we speak!

Everyone makes offers. It's a part of human nature. It's how we get what we want in life.

Some people are great at making offers, while others? Not so much.

Kids are great at offers. They know how to get what they want. "Mom, Mom! If you give me cookies I will stop nagging you. Just one cookie! Just one!"

Mom thinks, "For the tiny price of one cookie, I can get rid of this verbal harassment. Seems like a great offer."

And then, the bad offers.

A boy approaches a girl at the dance and says, "If you will dance with me ... uh ... uh ... uh." Yeah, that offer won't end well.

Or a man proposes to his girlfriend, "If you marry me, you get to keep the ring!" Hmmm. No comment.

So, what makes a great offer?

Here are a few ideas.

- It's an offer that uses a metaphor to create an "aha-moment" that hooks the other person.
- It's an offer that the other person cannot refuse.
- It's an offer that's so good, they would be crazy to say no!
- It's an offer that benefits both people involved.

- It's an offer that is fair.
- It's an offer with the intention of helping the other person, not just benefiting us.
- It's a clear offer. Not complicated or vague.

Let's think of more reasons some offers feel good, while others feel repulsive.

For instance, we love offers that are specific. Here are a few examples.

- "This idea can help you fire the boss."
- "Eat these special cookies–lose weight."
- "We will deliver a bucket of fried chicken to your door for $30."
- "Take these vitamins and feel great in the mornings."
- "Build a part-time business and use the money to retire early."
- "Use this special cream to get rid of wrinkles."
- "Make your skin so healthy you will never wear makeup again."
- "Come to our home for our Super Bowl party. We have snacks."

Do any of these offers sound familiar? They should.

We make or receive offers like these daily.

But, we are just warming up. We want to learn how to make spectacular, irresistible, awesome offers that our prospects can't refuse. Why?

Because our competition is tough! Our prospects hear good offers every day. We must stand out above the rest. We can't be ordinary.

Let's learn how to take our offer-making skills to a higher level, a place where we won't have competition.

But first?

A warning.

Our offers are not the most important factor when marketing to prospects.

There is a bigger "elephant in the room" factor we should talk about first. Let's get that "elephant in the room" out of the way now.

If we do this, then later, our improved offers will rock!

Let's go!

OUR OFFER IS NOT THE MOST IMPORTANT FACTOR

What? Really???

Whoa! This should be exciting.

Then, what is the #1 factor in successful offers?

The #1 most important factor is: We must have a good audience.

Our audience is way more important than the offer!!!

If our audience is unqualified, it won't matter how good our offer is, they will refuse it. Having eager, qualified prospects, wanting to buy, is the most important part of marketing. Examples?

Case study #1: Distributor Joe offers the best quality vitamins, at the best price, with a full money-back guarantee. The ingredients are picked from the freshest herbs in the Himalayan mountains by certified elves. The formulation doctor walks on water, does magic card tricks, and has an IQ of 251. And, a little-known organization awarded Joe's vitamins as their product of the year.

One problem. Joe is pitching his vitamins to the poorest Third World country that can't afford even basic food staples. Few can afford to buy his wonderful expensive vitamins. Even a 20% off coupon won't help.

Case study #2: A Chinese professor sells a Chinese-language grammar course. He talks to everyone in his local rural Texan community. No one wants it. No one speaks Chinese. There isn't even a Chinese restaurant in town. And who wants to take a trip to China anyway? They don't have Tex-Mex food. He has no audience or market. If this Chinese professor improves his offer to include streaming videos, it won't make a difference.

Case study #3: A beauty and skincare distributor targets men's rugby players in England. Their first priority? Beer and chips after the game. No player comments, "I worry about the fine lines around my bruised eye and broken nose." Well, maybe the rugby players need better skincare, but they don't want it. This will be a dead end, even if our skincare distributor includes a free eye-shadow bonus with every purchase.

Case study #4: The local kindergarten class.

Whoa! If that is our audience, we have some restrictions.

We can't sell booze and cigarettes to 5-year-olds. They don't even want them. Plus, I am sure their parents put a credit card limit restriction on their credit cards. No matter how good our offer is, no matter how big the discount, even the best of offers can't overcome a bad audience.

More case studies? What if we sold organic pet food, but our market was people who lived in apartments and condos that did not allow pets? Or, what if we were a luxury home builder, and our market was a small factory town where the factory just closed?

Okay, we get the idea. With an unqualified audience, even the best offer in the history of the world will fall on deaf ears.

A bad audience is terminal.

Instead of frustrating hard work trying to sell to an unqualified audience, let's reverse this principle and market to a qualified, eager audience. Let's see how easy this would be.

Good case study #1: A romantic gift distributor does smart targeting to sell her premium gifts. She goes to the local offices in her area one week before Valentine's Day. She asked the workers, "Have you purchased a romantic gift for your girlfriend or wife yet?" Of course, the answer is, "no." The workers panic as they mentally picture the scenario of not having a good gift on Valentine's Day.

Our romantic gift distributor continues, "Would you like me to take care of that for you?"

The office workers throw money at her, fighting to be first in line. Money is no object.

Does our romantic gift distributor have to offer a 10% off coupon for Valentine's Day to make the sale? No. When the audience is hungry, any offer will do.

Good case study #2: Sheila sells a magic fat burning weight loss pill. She locates a local weight-loss group that is holding a contest. She asked, "Who wants an edge over your competitors?" Many of the competitors put down their pizza, raise their donut-stained fingers, and say, "Me! Me! Me!"

This wasn't hard at all. Did Sheila have to enhance her offer? No. She didn't have to give them a 10% off coupon for a weight loss shake. This was a hungry market wanting to buy now.

Good case study #3: Weight-loss selling on steroids.

I wrote about this in our book, "51 Ways and Places to Sponsor New Distributors." This is one of my favorite campaigns. Here is what happened.

While eating Mexican food with distributors from a workshop, I asked the lady across the table what she sold. She answered, "I sell diet products."

To continue the conversation, I asked, "So how is it going?"

She told me, "I am so tired. Every day I deliver boxes and boxes of my diet products to customers all over the city. This is exhausting."

Now, I am thinking, "That is pretty incredible. She must have a secret. Maybe the diet products are a bargain or something."

So I asked her, "Well, how much do these diet products cost?"

She said, "Well, the cheapest package is $350 for a month's supply, but I normally sell the $600 packs."

I now think, "$600 a pack? I could buy 300 baskets of these tortilla chips for that. That is expensive for a month of diet products. How could she sell that many packs so easily?" But, I kept my composure and posture.

I then asked, "So tell me. Where do you find these prospects for those expensive $600 diet packs? Let me know and maybe I could give you some advice or a tip or two."

She said:

"I go to bridal shows and talk to the brides-to-be. When I ask them if they want to lose a little weight before the wedding, they instantly say 'Yes.' This is their big day. No matter how anorexic-looking the bride-to-be appears, every bride wants to lose just a little more weight before their special day.

"The average wedding costs between $20,000 and $50,000 here. The $600 diet pack isn't even a thought, it is barely a tip. So the bride-to-be orders immediately, no questions asked.

"But then the bride's mother decides that she wants to lose weight too. She doesn't want to look fat in those wedding pictures for the rest of eternity. She orders her pack.

"And so does the future mother-in-law. She doesn't want to be the fat one in the picture.

"And then, the bridesmaids. They are going to look awful in those off-color dresses they have to wear to make the bride look pretty. They don't want to look awful and fat. They order too.

"So I load up my car with as many packs as I can, and I spend the entire day delivering and talking to my new, enthusiastic customers."

Needless to say, I didn't give her any advice or tips.

"Who sells to my prospects?"

If we have a qualified, hungry, and desperate audience, we don't have to be very good. Even a minimal offer sells. And sales skills? Not needed when people want to buy.

If there is one giant step to sales success, it would be, "Find a hungry audience who wants to buy."

Everything else is simple.

So, what is more important?

1. Having a hungry audience who wants to buy?

2. An incredible offering?

The answer is obvious.

We want hungry buyers. Let's do an example.

Overweight people at the donut shop.

Imagine we sold weight-loss products. As a donut-eating expert, I pay attention to my fellow donut fans. We enjoy donuts. All kinds of donuts. In fact, we love donuts.

Then wouldn't the donut shop be the perfect place to locate people that need to lose weight? Everyone in the donut shop needs to lose weight. Finding people who need what we have to offer? Easy.

Ah. But that is the problem. No one is going to the donut shop to lose weight. These are terrible prospects. As donut groupies we desperately need to lose weight.

But ... but ... do we want to lose weight?

No.

That is why we are at the donut shop and not at the gym. We tell ourselves, "Oh, I need to lose weight." However, inside our minds we make a daily decision to eat more delicious donuts.

We need to lose weight, but we don't want to lose weight.

Now it starts to get obvious.

So where would we find weight-challenged prospects who want to lose weight? Easy.

First, we would look for chubby people in the gym.

Second, we would look for calorie-enhanced, jiggling walkers on the jogging trail.

Third, we would stand by the weight-loss section in the local book store.

Fourth, we ask for referrals from the shoe salesman at the mall. We say, "If someone asks for walking shoes so they can start exercising, and if they are a bit chubby, could you tell them to call me for help?"

This is much, much easier.

We don't want prospects who need to lose weight. Our market is only with the prospects who want to lose weight now.

When we understand the difference of "needs versus wants", we will now locate the best prospects.

Plus, our new team members will be talking to high-quality prospects who want to take immediate action. This is a better experience for everyone.

Bottom line?

Start now. Find our audience, the people who want what we're offering. Selling ice cubes to Eskimos is hard work. Our time is valuable.

Find our audience, the qualified prospects who want and can afford what we have to offer. Then, make our offer. For example we could say, "Would you rather try the easy way or the hard way to lose weight?"

Don't start with enhancing our offer and hope for buyers to magically appear.

A good audience comes first.

Let's make great offers to people who (and here is the secret word) … WANT what we have to offer.

There is a huge difference between needs and wants. If our new team members don't understand the difference, expect frustration and poor results.

So let's figure out this "needs and wants" thinking in our prospects.

DON'T GET THIS WRONG

We should look for people who need what we offer, right?

Fatal mistake.

A common mistake.

We don't want to add ourselves to the pile of dead corpses that confused "needs" and "wants" in their short-lived career.

Needs vs. Wants

What are needs? What are wants?

Well, I need to eat healthy, but I don't want to.

What do I want?

Donuts. Pizza. Cake and cookies. Okay, I also want ice cream.

Because I eat this unhealthy diet, I **need** to lose weight. But, I don't **want** to lose weight because I hate the feeling of being hungry. I **want** to feel full.

So what happens? I get fatter. And out of shape. So I **need** to exercise. But I don't **want** to exercise, as I am allergic to exercise. Every time I exercise my heart races and I break out into a sweat. That can't be healthy.

Instead of exercising, I **want** to watch television and surf the Internet. Yes, that is what I really **want**.

I don't **need** to eat three more pieces of birthday cake, but I **want** to. Chocolate cake is my favorite. With an extra layer of chocolate frosting.

You might think that I **need** willpower. Sure. But, I don't **want** to have willpower. I don't **want** to give up all of the things that I **want**. In fact, I am feeling pretty great without willpower.

I **need** to visit the dentist every year, but I don't **want** to. No one enjoys dental pain.

The list can go on, but we get the idea.

Now it is clear

Needs are things we have to do, but don't necessarily want to do. We need basic things such as food, clothing, housing, laundry, waking up early for work, and preparing our taxes. Too often we procrastinate and put off what we need to do. Sound familiar?

Wants are things we would like to do, but don't have to do. This sounds like more fun. We don't require extra motivation or lectures for our wants. We want the weekends to come sooner, more scoring by our favorite sports teams, and can't wait for the next blockbuster movie of our favorite characters.

If there is something we want, personal motivation is not a problem. We are ready to go.

Test our understanding

I am fat. I need to lose weight, but I don't want the pain and suffering that comes from the denial of my favorite foods. So here are my choices:

Choice #1: Enjoy a delicious piece of rich chocolate cake, smothered in ice cream and topped with sweet whipped cream. And … smile.

Choice #2: Don't eat. Suffer excruciating stomach pains. Feel irritable and mean. And possibly fall into a deep depression.

Hmmm. What choice do you think is easiest for me?

And this explains why selling what people "need" is the pathway to ruin

Okay, a bit dramatic, but we now see how hard it is to sell what people need.

People are not dumb. They know what they need. But they act on what they want. People have to take action to buy.

So if we want to make a great network marketing offer to our prospects, let's think about what people want.

Bottom line?

Needs are boring and wants are fun!

What does this mean for us who make sales, influence people to follow a cause, or want to persuade people into action?

We can be more successful when we present our offers as a "want" instead of a "need."

Think "positioning." Even if we offer something people need, by positioning or describing it as a want, we will get more people to agree.

Make it sound fun. Make it sound exciting. Make our offer so appealing that people can't help but say, "Yes!"

The most natural mistake when we begin?

Easy.

Our logical minds default to, "Let's make my offer to people who NEED what I offer."

It doesn't end well.

Frustrations, objections, wasted time, and crushing reminders of our failures will chip away at our belief in what we offer.

Sounds grim.

So what is a quick solution? How can we retrain our minds?

With a story.

This important story is easy to remember. It will help us keep our belief in what we offer while helping us find the best prospects for our business.

How about a practical example? Ready?

Failed distributor's last words

"I will find people who need my products."

Yes, pretty dumb. A sure path to failure. Lots of people need our products, but don't want them. They are not our market. They won't buy what we sell.

Our market is with people who want what we have to offer. People buy their wants and avoid buying their needs.

Let's imagine you sell diet products. Who needs your products? Fat people!

You go to the local donut shop and see me sitting on two stools filling my face with donuts. Naturally, you try to sell me your diet products.

Yes, I need to lose weight. But, do I want to? Of course not. That is why I am in the donut shop, filling my face with donuts. I need to lose weight, but I want to eat donuts.

But let's change the scene. Here is a picture of me trying to figure out how to jump over a rope. Obviously, I am an amateur, but at least I am trying. I need to lose weight, and I also want to lose weight.

Selling your diet products to me will be much easier.

So, does that mean that we should never approach poor people with our business opportunities?

No. What this means is, "It is not where someone is in life that matters. What matters is whether they want to go somewhere else."

So yes, some poor people want to spend their lives on TikTok. Other poor people may want to have a chance to build their financial future.

So, does that mean we should only approach rich people with our business opportunities?

No. If a rich person is happy where he is, he won't want to look at our opportunity.

We need to find people who want something better. It doesn't matter how much money they have, it is only important that they want something more.

Remember this: People buy their wants and avoid buying their needs! That is the key to effective marketing–finding those who want what we offer.

JOE'S STORY BEGINS ...
BADLY

"Whoa, check out these products and services. Everybody in my family is gonna want to buy these." Our prospect, Joe, can't believe what he is seeing. Our opportunity meeting is the door to his future riches.

Joe begins to drool. Dollar signs form in his eyes. He begins to dream.

"When I get home, I am sure there will be a line at my door to buy from me. My family and friends will just have to wait in line. Maybe I'll give them a number in the queue. They will have wads of cash in their hands, ready to buy. How could anyone turn my new business offer down? I am going to be rich! I can smell the gas fumes of my future Lamborghini even now."

As the opportunity meeting continues, Joe begins to hyperventilate. His body vibrates with excitement.

"I can't believe this generous compensation plan! Look at all the money that we can earn. My loser friends at work will faint when they see it. They will mob my desk. I see them throwing money at me already. They know they are underpaid. They can't wait to fire our boss and be their own boss. This is their chance to get the money they need. I will break records for the fastest-growing group ever."

Joe dreams past hyper-positive and delusional. But, he doesn't stop there.

"My friends at work will tell their relatives, who tell their relatives, who tell their relatives, and I will qualify for the Presidential Gold Ambassador Eagle with Extra Feathers rank in a week! Everyone needs to earn extra money, so how hard could this be?"

Life is good when we have positive prospects like Joe.

Remember when we first saw our network marketing business opportunity? Can we remember when we were in Joe's shoes? Our minds were racing. We convinced ourselves that everyone would see exactly what we see, an amazing opportunity.

And then, reality happens

What kind of reception do you think Joe receives from his family and friends? What do you think they tell him? Something like this?

"Are you crazy? Did you fall on your head? What are you smoking? Are you taking drugs? Did your brain lobotomy go wrong? What makes you think I would fall for some pyramid scheme? I am not a salesman. I don't do these sorts of things. You are now officially banned from weddings and funerals. Not only is this idea stupid, but I never did like you."

Joe's prospects eagerly club his motivational spirit into submission. They beat out all positivity from his brain. Joe gets humiliated, rejected, insulted, and ghosted. It feels as though he is the target in a human shooting gallery. Joe's dreams of being rich and famous vanish in a sad puff of smoke.

"100% rejection by everyone! Maybe I made a big mistake joining this opportunity."

Joe convinces himself that he will never sponsor anyone. He doesn't need more proof. His battle scars prove this business is not possible.

Defeated. Embarrassed. Depressed.

"I will go home, hide underneath my sofa, grab the remote control, and watch television for the rest of my life. No need to show my face in public again. What was I thinking? I joined a lousy opportunity that no one wants. This was a bad, bad decision. If my stupid, con artist sponsor calls, I will block his number."

One more try

While crying on his pizza, Joe thinks. "Well, maybe my relatives and friends don't have much vision in their lives. They only talk about soccer practice and drinking beer on weekends anyway. I never realized they were so useless. But at least my friends at work still have a spark of life in them. Let's see if they will react better."

At work the next day, Joe makes his big announcement.

"Hey guys, I have this great business opportunity that you will love. It is perfect for us as we are all looking to make some extra money. This is our chance to fire the boss, be our own boss, and finally get the financial freedom we always wanted."

Joe's co-workers laugh at him and call him a loser. They grind in their negative feelings by saying:

* "We are calling security!"

* "Are you insane? "

* "Never bother or talk to us again!"

* "We are only 44 years away from retirement. Don't you do anything to mess that up!"

* "Why can't you be happy with that 2% annual raise they promised to give us next year?"
* "When did this pyramid fall on your head?"
* "Get off your happy drugs prescription and join reality."
* "Resign yourself to a lifetime of labor. Get over it!"

Joe gets humiliated and convinced that he should never talk to anyone again. Why can't his co-workers see the opportunity? They need it. Everyone complains about the dream-sucking vampire boss who takes little bits of their brains out every day turning them into human zombies. Why can't they see it???

It was a lonely trip home that day. While driving, Joe thought about his options. "This is worse than being the butt of the joke in high school. Why don't I give up? I could call my sponsor six months from now and say that I talked to everyone, no one wanted to join, and I quit. That sounds like a plan. But, I got credit card debt, I'm behind on my mortgage payments, and the bank is threatening to repossess my car, so I better do something. I will give this one more try."

Online!

Joe's new plan? Online and social media, of course.

Joe reasons, "If friends, family, and coworkers are useless, why not talk to strangers? No one will criticize me online, as no one knows me. Let me go further into credit card debt, run a few online ads, and reap the profits."

Uh-oh.

We know how this ends. Anonymous strangers love criticizing, so Joe's self-image takes a beating. There is a principle in network marketing that goes like this: "If our friends and relatives hate what we say, then strangers aren't going to like it any better!"

A cloud of deep depression forms over Joe's head. This isn't what Joe envisioned.

Did we ever sponsor a new team member like Joe? And did our new team have the same bad experience as Joe? What about us? Did we experience rejection when we started?

Who is at fault?

Okay, something bad happened here. But, who is at fault?

Were Joe's friends, family, and co-workers at fault? No.

Was social media the evil villain in this story? No.

Well, what about Joe? Joe was at the scene of the crime every time. So is this Joe's fault? No.

Well, we have to blame someone. How about the company? The economy? The squirrels in the park? No.

The incompetent, malicious villain in the story is … Joe's sponsor!

Joe's sponsor???

Joe is brand new to the business. How many skills of network marketing would Joe know? Zero? No one taught Joe network marketing skills in school, his parents didn't, and his job didn't either. Joe is clueless about how the real world works.

Then who is going to get Joe started?

His sponsor!

Sure, Joe can learn skills as he goes along in his network marketing career, but he won't have any skills when he starts. Joe's sponsor can give him a head start.

One of the most important stories for Joe to hear is the story of "Needs vs. Wants." This story explains how humans think.

Spoiler alert! People don't think logically, rationally, and seldom intelligently. Human brains are messed up with bad programming, cognitive biases, and emotional reactions.

Logical and rational stuff is what we think about.

But when it comes to action, it is our emotions and expectations that instigate action. Our motivation to act comes from our brain's internal emotions.

If we expect humans to act rationally and logically, we are in for a big surprise. Need proof? Watch soap operas on television. The drama and action come from emotions.

So what is this magical "Needs vs. Wants" story?

This simple story helps new network marketers understand and anticipate the reactions of their prospects. No surprises.

When is the better time to take care of a future objection? Now. With our simple "Needs vs. Wants" story, we can immunize our new team members from the future reactions of their prospects.

Before we learn the story, pretend for a moment that we are a brand new team member hearing the story for the very first time. After hearing the story, ask yourself, "Would I have benefitted to hear this story immediately upon enrolling?"

But let's get to the story now.

In this example story, we will pretend that we sell nutritional supplements. But please, substitute any product or service for your version of this powerful story.

Ready?

THE "NEEDS VS. WANTS" STORY BEGINS

We tell Joe this story.

Let's begin.

There is a huge difference between needs and wants

People need things, but don't want them.

That is normal. Don't feel surprised that humans act like … humans.

Some examples?

- Everybody needs to visit the dentist every year, but do they want to? Nooooooo! That hurts. We want to put off dentist appointments as long as possible.

- Everybody should wake up an hour early every morning and go jogging and exercise. But do we want to? Nooooooo! We want to sleep in. It feels better.

- Everybody needs to diet and eat healthy foods, but do they want to? Nooooooo! We want to eat fast food, pizza, donuts, … and candy? Oh my! That is the best!

- Everybody needs to pay their taxes. But, do we want to? Nooooooo! We want to delay and put off preparing our taxes for as long as possible.
- Everybody needs to save for retirement, but do they want to? Nooooooo! We would rather spend our money on lottery tickets today.
- Everybody needs to go to bed at a decent time, but do they want to? Nooooooo! We want to watch one more episode of our favorite show or stay up chatting with friends. Parties are fun!

So, it is perfectly normal for people to need things, but don't want them. Does that seem normal to you?

So, when you get home you'll be talking to your aunt. Your Aunt Mary will say, "My ankle hurts. My hip hurts. My back hurts. My shoulder hurts. My neck hurts. I have migraine headaches. I have acid reflux, and you know that is a disease now. I have five known diseases, four unknown diseases, and three diseases they haven't even discovered yet!"

And when your aunt finally takes a breath, you will ask, "Do you want to do something about it?"

"Nooooooooooooooo! My children visit me more when I pretend to be sick. I see the doctor every week and it feels like a social visit. I get my aerobic exercise from opening prescription jars. Don't you dare suggest I do anything to fix this! If I were to feel well, I wouldn't have anything to complain about or talk about. What would I say to my friends?"

Well, Aunt Mary needs our nutritional products, but she doesn't want them. In fact, she is looking to get one more illness to one-up her neighbor, Helen. Who can suffer the most is a competition in her neighborhood.

You see, people need things, but don't want them. This is normal. Don't feel surprised that people are just like us. They need to do things, but don't want to do those very same things. Don't worry. It just means they will wait longer until they have no other choice.

And tomorrow, when you go to work, you might talk to your co-workers about this business opportunity. In conversation, they will complain, "My daughter needs braces for her teeth, and my car broke down. I am behind on my credit cards, and I can't make my mortgage payments. I asked the boss for a raise and he refused. I desperately need some extra money fast."

What will you say to them? "

You'll smile and say, "Do you want to do something about it?" Their reply?

"Nooooooooooooooo! Nothing works for me. I am a professional victim. Somebody in China lost money once. I can't sell. I don't know anyone. I lost my graduation list. I don't have a Christmas card list. I just moved into my neighborhood. I am not a salesman! No time! I don't know anyone! Getting underpaid every month is building my character. I want to fall on a sword, but I can't get anyone to hold the sword for me."

Well, our co-workers need extra money, but do they want it? Not really. They prefer to wait until they have no other choice in their lives. For now, marathon television evenings and lazy weekends are what they want.

Relax. Our co-workers are normal. They need what we have to offer, but they don't want it now. Don't feel surprised when you see this. Instead, wait until the time is right for them. We would want the same courtesy in our lives. When people don't want to buy or join now, it doesn't mean they are bad people. It just isn't their time.

Always remember this.

Our business is not with people who need what we offer. Our business is only with people who want what we offer.

Our story with our new team member continues.

Think of the situation like this. What is the best restaurant here in the city?

The Ace Gourmet Diner. They have the best steaks in the country.

Does everybody need to try their steaks? Yes! They are awesome! The steaks are so tender you can eat them with a spoon. They will even cook the steaks in 49 different ways. And, their staff is so nice. They all have hospitality awards. And we must get in line early. There is always a line waiting to get a table.

Now, does everyone here in the city need to go there and try their steaks? Yes! But do they want to? Nooooooo!

And why not? They will have many reasons why they don't want to go to the Ace Gourmet Diner.

- They heard the waiter dropped a steak once. Terrible.
- There is a long waiting time to get into the restaurant.
- Traffic is bad on that side of town.
- There is no place to park close by.
- The portions aren't big enough.

- Some people are vegetarians.
- Don't like the color of their uniforms.
- Eating with chopsticks is more fun.
- Too expensive.
- Prefer fried chicken instead.
- They heard someone cut their finger on the menu.
- The menu needs more variety of potato dishes.
- And the list goes on.

The reality? 99% of the people in our city don't want to go to the Ace Gourmet Diner.

But ... they have a great business with the 1% of the people who want to come!

The same is true in our network marketing business.

If 99% of the people don't want to join our team. That's okay! We only need the 1% who do want to join our team. So, when you talk to your co-workers, friends, and family about your new business opportunity, don't worry about the 99% who don't want to join your team. They are not your market!

Here is an important lesson for us. Don't try to convince the 99% to do something they don't want to do. It doesn't work.

For example, think about the Ace Gourmet Diner. They know their business is with the 1% who want to come. You won't see their waiters out in the street with menus forcing people inside. They don't insist that people walking past must attend an opportunity meeting about their entrées. They don't force people to watch a video about the restaurant. They don't even have conference calls about their appetizers. They know their business is with the 1% who want to come, and they have a wonderful business.

So think about the 1% who want to do business with us. Our job is to let people know about our business, and if they are the 1%, they will volunteer. We don't have to force them or sell them to join. When the time is right for them, they will see what we see, a great opportunity.

Here's a memorable way to look at it

Imagine you had a job to find people named … Bob. You approach me and say, "Hey Sponsor, what is your name?"

I answer, "Sponsor."

Then you say, "Well, don't you want to be named Bob? It would be easier for me if your name was Bob. You kind of look like a Bob. Do you feel like a Bob? Hey, here is a form to change your name to Bob. Can you please be a Bob?"

Would you do that? Of course not. You would simply look for someone else and see if their name was Bob.

Or, if you wanted to be more efficient you could try this. You could ask me, "Do you know anyone named Bob?" If I did, I could point you in their direction.

I might reply, "Yes, my best friend's name is Bob. Plus, I have a co-worker named Bob. And both of my brothers are named … Bob!"

Now you can point your efforts to talk to these recommended Bobs. These are your perfect prospects.

Our network marketing business is similar to locating people named Bob. Not everyone has to be named Bob. Our business would only be with people named Bob.

Do we wish our sponsor told us this story when we started?

This would have saved us a lot of grief, and a lot of hurt feelings. We would have been more polite with the people we talked to.

When new team members don't know the story, they take rejection personally. It lowers their self-image. They feel something is wrong with them, or with the opportunity. They don't realize that people are acting normal.

Humans do things they want to. Trying to sell them or convince them to do otherwise not only irritates them. This wastes time that could be better spent looking for the 1% who want what we offer.

Memorizing this story is easy with this little outline

Part #1: How people are normal when they avoid what they need to do, and instead, do what they want to do.

Part #2: What will happen when they get home and talk to their normal family and friends?

Part #3: What will happen when they talk to their co-workers?

Part #4: Our favorite restaurant example.

Part #5: It is like finding people named Bob.

Part #1 of the story describes how humans avoid things they need to do. If our new team member doesn't believe it, we can make an example that's more personal. We could ask if our new team member wants to wake up one hour earlier in the morning to go jogging. The answer? "Uh, no. Yes, I probably need to exercise more, but I don't want to."

Now, let's make this story stick in the mind of our new team member. We could say this.

"Well, the next day I corner you at work and insist that you commit to waking up an hour early to jog with me the next day. How would you feel? Not good. And what if I brought my sponsor along with me and we both tried to convince you? How would you feel about that? And the next day, I give you a magazine about jogging. And the next day I recommend a motivational audio about jogging. And finally, every morning I follow up with you early to ask if you changed your mind. How would you feel?"

Ouch. Our new team member now has empathy for the prospects who need to do something, but don't want to.

Part #2 describes how family and friends need our products and services, but don't want them. Here is our chance to customize this part of the story to our products and services.

For example, imagine we sold discount mobile phone services. We could describe how a relative might say this, "My phone bill went up again on renewal!" So of course, we asked, "Would you like to do something about it? And the answer? "Nooooooo! My brother was ripped off by the Mega Phone Corporation. My father was overcharged by the Mega Phone Corporation. And yes, even my grandfather paid too much for his Mega Phone Corporation monthly billing. And me? I want to be ripped off just like them! I believe in loyalty."

The bigger the exaggeration, the better.

Or, if we sell skincare, we could describe a relative saying this, "I have flaky skin over here. My skin is dry over there. The oily spot is here. And, I have wrinkles so deep I can store food in them!"

When a relative finally takes a breath from complaining, we ask, "Would you like to do something about it?" And the answer?

"Nooooooo! I love that greasy spot on my forehead. It makes my hat slip on so much easier. And the flaky skin? It accumulates on the sofa. Every time I sit on the sofa it looks like a snowstorm. Reminds me of my youth in New Hampshire. I want to keep my wrinkles. They make me look so sophisticated. Oh, and stop bothering me. I never did like you."

There is no need to put down their relatives and friends who are not interested. They are just being normal.

Part #3 of the story describes how the co-workers might respond to the business opportunity. Here is where we can have some fun. Everyone knows at least one negative, dream-stealing employee. We describe what our new team member will hear when introducing the opportunity to co-workers.

"So, you want me to what? No way! I don't like change. I'm comfortable here. Why would I want to work for myself? I'm already working hard to make our boss rich. You should give up on your business! What makes you so special that you feel you can dream about a different future? Everyone needs to commute and fight traffic every day anyway. Gives us time to listen to depressing country music. And by the way, you're going to fail. I give you two weeks before you're apologizing to me for trying to improve your life."

Our new team member thinks, "Yeah, I can see Sam at work saying this right now. He gave up hope in his life years ago."

Part #4: Our favorite restaurant example.

Don't have a favorite restaurant in your city? Or maybe our new team member can't relate to restaurants? Then, let's use a different example to illustrate that a business can become successful with only a tiny percentage of the market.

How about an example of a luxury BMW dealership?

We could say this to our new team member:

"Imagine that you owned a BMW dealership. Now, most people would love to, because they are very profitable automobiles to sell. But, not everyone wants to buy a BMW automobile, right? Well, 99% of the people in our city would rather buy a Toyota, a Mercedes, a Ford, a Chevrolet, or even a Porsche. Yes, 99% of people don't want what you have to offer. Your business is only with the 1% that want to purchase a BMW automobile. And that is okay. You will still have a wonderful business with the tiny 1% of people who want what you offer. And, you don't have to spend any time or energy trying to convince the 99% of people who don't want a BMW. You will be very successful with only 1% of the market. You would spend your time looking for the 1% who want a BMW, not with the 99% who don't."

Part #5: It is like finding people named Bob.

This part of our story should convince our new team member to avoid trying to change people. Using the Bob example is funny. It helps our team member remember the story. Remember, the more ridiculous we can make the story, the more it will stick in our team member's mind. Here are more ideas to enhance our story.

"Imagine your business was to find people named … Bob. Every day you wished your good friend, Mike, had parents that would have named him Bob. But his parents didn't. What would you do? Would you invite Mike to a name-changing workshop? Would you try to hypnotize and trick Mike into thinking his name was Bob? Would you secretly change Mike's passport and driver's license so his name would appear as Bob? Would you spend the rest of your life mispronouncing Mike's name as 'Bob' instead? Would you hope to support a political candidate that would change the laws so that everyone had to change their name to Bob? Of course not. We would just get on with our business trying to locate people named, Bob.

"The good news is that when we find someone named, Bob, we don't have to high-pressure or convince that person to buy or join. We would spend our time asking people if they knew anyone named, Bob. If we were speaking to an audience of 100 people, we would ask if anyone in the audience was named Bob. We wouldn't stress or get upset that other people didn't want to change their names. Why? Because our business is only with people named Bob."

Let's take this lesson personally

We want to respect our prospects' decisions. There are many reasons now may not be the best time for them. This is normal.

Our business is only with the people that want what we have to offer … now.

We wish we had heard the "Bob" story early in our careers. Prospects rejected us as we forced our agenda on them. We didn't respect the timing in their lives.

Our prospects aren't stupid. They know they need what we offer. But at this moment, they may have a different agenda in their lives.

Forcing ourselves onto others sounds like this.

Imagine our best friend is a fitness coach. He calls us at 5 a.m. Ouch. He says, "Let's go jogging."

We groan and stutter, "Let me sleep."

But that doesn't stop our best friend. No. Why?

Because he listened to a motivational audio at 4:30 am that morning. He reviewed his vision board. He pumped up his enthusiasm with five minutes of jumping jacks in front of the mirror while telling himself, "I am one with the universe! I have a great attitude. Prosperity and positive feelings flow through my entire being."

As our best friend is attempting to sell us on an early morning jog, what are we thinking?

"No!"

We turn off our telephone and go back to sleep.

Later that morning we see our best friend at work. He tells us, "You got to come jogging with me tomorrow. I will bring my sponsor with me. We can talk about the value of exercise while we are jogging. I have new information about the health benefits of jogging. And when we finish, I can show you a company video of other people jogging."

How do we feel about this? We still don't want to go jogging.

But our best friend doesn't give up. The next day at work he asks us to subscribe to his company's jogging magazine. He says, "I know the magazine will inspire you. Plus, every morning I will call you up at 5 a.m." He hopes his persistence will wear us down. Just keep following up!

Will we change our minds? No.

So let's remember this example before we make fun of our relatives for not wanting to join us now.

Let's remember how we felt at 5 a.m. in the morning. We are normal. We needed to jog and exercise, but we did not want to.

Every day we see examples of prospects needing what we offer, but not wanting it.

Do any of these examples seem familiar?

Aunt Connie.

At a party, we have a nice conversation with our Aunt Connie. But soon it deteriorates and she says, "I need a vacation. I am so stressed out. The people at work are morons. My relatives gossip about me all day. And friends? All they do is ask for favors! I have to get away! Far away! Maybe to a beach, sit alone, 500 miles from everybody I know."

So we say to Aunt Connie, "So Auntie, do you want to do something about it?"

And she replies, "Oh no. They need me at work. My niece's piano concert is in two weeks. I sunburn too easily. Those holidays are too expensive for my budget. I will stay with my sister-in-law again like last year. I will buy a six-pack of allergy drugs as I am allergic to her 32 cats."

Aunt Connie needs our discounted travel holiday product to keep her sanity. However, does she want what we offer? No. For her, it is easier to give up her dream holiday and resign to a week at her sister-in-law's cat commune.

Aunt Connie is a perfect example of people needing a solution, but they don't want the solution.

Our aunt is human. She is normal.

Uncle Steve.

Our uncle complains, "I got ripped off by my electricity company. They overcharged me three times already. Customer service sends me to a minimum-wage employee from a foreign country that has no access to my account. And then my call gets transferred to voicemail!"

So we say, "Uncle Steve, would you like to do something about it?"

He replies, "I am not trying anything new! This electric company ripped off my grandfather, ripped off my father, and I want to be ripped off just like them. I tried change in 1969. It didn't work out then, and I don't want to try it again."

So will our uncle change? No. Our uncle needs to change, but does he want to? No.

Aunt Judy.

Our other aunt complains, "It is impossible for me to lose weight. I eat from the four basic food groups, Italian, Mexican, French, and Chinese, and I still gain weight. They say we should eat a variety of foods, but that puts on more weight. Stupid advice. And then I switched to donuts. They have holes in the middle, so they should be less calories, right? Did I lose weight? Nooooo! So I started eating chocolate-covered donuts to at least get the antioxidant value from the chocolate. But no matter what I do, I can't lose weight."

Our Aunt Judy definitely needs our super diet capsules. But does she want them? We better check.

We ask our aunt, "Auntie, do you want to do something about it? Would you like some super diet capsules to help with these problems?"

Our aunt replies, "No! No! They might be unsafe and I value my health. Plus I am allergic to everything in a capsule. I can't swallow capsules or liquids. I need approval from my doctor before I make a decision to be healthy. And the extra fat around my waist protects my vital organs. Keep those healthy capsules away from me!"

Okay, we got the hint. Our aunt is one of the millions of people that could use our super diet capsules, but she doesn't want to. She is not our market.

Why the "needs vs wants" story is so important

If we don't immunize and educate our new team members, they will be shocked by prospects' reactions. They will think there is something wrong with themselves or the opportunity. They will have a feeling of dread that they made a bad decision to join our business. They will avoid talking to people. This story helps explains why there is nothing wrong with other people's reactions. They are just being normal.

Now, our new team member will think, "These people are normal. I don't jog at 5 AM in the morning either. People do what they want to do, not what they need to do."

"But this person could be great in my business!"

Yes, many people have the talent and connections to be awesome in network marketing. However, they don't want to do it. They have other goals or priorities in their lives. The "want" is the most important part of prospecting.

Here is what will happen if we don't explain the "wants" part of the "needs vs wants" story.

Our team member will send us to dead-end appointments with people who could be great in our business, but don't want to do it. Here are two examples of these types of unqualified prospects.

We get a call from our new team member. "You won't believe this! You got to come with me as I have the best prospect ever. My cousin has a neighbor who knows someone who had an uncle who had a friend that used to be famous in sports. He is retired now, but everyone knows him. He knows everybody. He is so busy signing autographs and posting on social media, it was difficult to get an appointment. But, I have an appointment from 2:10 PM to 2:16 PM next Thursday with his press agent."

Got the bad feeling yet?

Does this famous athlete need more money to pay his rent? After his millions of dollars of sponsorship money, probably not.

Uh, this doesn't look good, so we ask our new team member, "Does this famous ex-athlete want to do our business? Does he want a change in his life?"

"Uh, well, uh ... I haven't really talked to him, but he could be good."

Our new team member slows down and thinks of what he said.

Many prospects could be awesome in our business. They have influence. They are famous. They have a natural market of prospects.

But do these prospects want to do our business? No.

Our business is not with people that need what we want, could be good at our business, or even people that have lots of contacts. Our business is with people that "want" what we offer.

Ready for another time-wasting example?

Do we know who would be awesome at our business? The person that would reach the top rank in one evening? Well, that would be the president of the United States. All the president needs to do is send out an announcement to all the government employees. "There is an opportunity meeting at the White House on Tuesday night, 7 PM. Be there if you want to keep your job."

Well, the President of the United States needs our business, but doesn't want it right now. Why?

The president might say, "Sure, I will need some residual income. This job runs out soon. But hey, I got some other things I must do now. Got this election campaign picking up speed. Plus those pesky enemies of our nation take up so much of my time. And since I was elected to oversee things, each day I need every waking moment and every ounce of energy to manage my 9,000,000 workers."

Let's get over it.

Instead, let's laser-focus our business on people who want what we have to offer.

Now, for the second most important lesson in making successful offers.

This lesson is called, "Head Trash!"

HEAD TRASH- THE #2 FACTOR

Okay. The #1 most important thing, more important than our offer, is … having a good audience.

If we have a great audience of potential buyers, we won't have to make superhuman offers or have ninja persuasion skills. Our great audience of potential buyers will be forgiving. They just want a good offer to solve their problems.

But let's improve our chances. Ready?

What is the #2 factor in making great offers?

Our personal thoughts and internal programs.

This is our personal head trash.

Oh.

So even with a good audience, our head trash can get in the way.

How?

First, our head trash tells us that we are salespeople. We are in a live/die, win/lose, make a sale/get rejected situation. This creates fear and we hesitate. What a motivation killer.

Second, if we believe we are in a live/die, win/lose, make a sale/ get rejected situation, ... then this will project our agenda to our prospect. Yes, our prospects can sense our agenda. How?

- They read our body language
- They listen to our tone of voice
- They observe our micro-facial expressions
- They judge the words we say

Our agenda to make a sale will cause our prospects to be defensive. Now they will look for reasons why our offer won't work, so that they have some objections to protect themselves from our high-pressure close.

Yes, we cause our prospects to look for reasons why our offer won't work. This doesn't end well.

Humans are experts at reading other humans' intentions. Need examples?

- We know when someone starts a sales pitch
- We prejudge strangers in seconds
- We know from our spouse's tone of voice if something is wrong
- We sense if someone "looks" untrustworthy
- We feel our friend's conversation is leading up to a request for a loan

We can't keep our thoughts and agenda secret. People know.

So, if people know and react to our sales agenda, what should we do?

Change our agenda!

When we change our intention, everything changes. And then our prospects will react to our new agenda.

Done. Easy. Solved.

Uh yeah, but what should we change our agenda to?

How about this?

Here are 10 things we can do to instantly change our agenda

#1. Our mission is not to sell prospects what they don't want.

#2. We don't want to manipulate people into our agenda.

#3. What we offer is an improvement for our prospects' lives. We don't have to convince them.

#4. We are not asking a favor or asking them to buy.

#5. Prospects know their personal situation far better than we do.

#6. Our job is to get our prospects to hear what we have to offer.

#7. Prospects are saying "yes" to us when they agree to a conversation.

#8. Prospects say "no" to an offer, not to us personally.

#9. Prospects say "no" because of their current personal circumstances.

#10. We are not in charge of our prospects' decisions and choices in life. We didn't choose their spouses or their jobs.

So, instead of trying to sell and convince our prospect of what we offer, instead, let's …

Gift one more option for our prospects' lives!

And how will our prospect react to our new agenda?

"An option? That means I have a choice. I am in charge. I get to choose. No sales pressure. I don't have to take this option. I can look at this option to see if it fits into my current situation. But, the only way for me to benefit from this option, is to find something good in the option that will improve my life. Let me look for something good in what you are about to offer."

Wow!

A big change in our prospects' reaction to us.

Feel the difference between these two phrases:

- A sales presentation
- An additional option

Totally different feeling, right? People love options.

Now, when we present our offer as an option to our prospects, we remove resistance and skepticism. We remove our personal agenda to sell. Our prospects can accept our offer with an open mind, and then weigh our offer in light of their current situation.

Current situation?

Yes, our prospects know their exact situation. We don't.

We don't know if they had a fight with their spouse one hour before meeting us. We don't know the current balance in their checking account. We don't know what other outside pressures are more important to them now.

The reality?

We have no idea what people are dealing with in their personal lives right now. Time for us to be respectful.

When we pre-judge, and assume we know their situation, this can make us look like egotistical, pompous jerks. Instead, we will honor their intelligence, and let them decide if our option can improve their lives now, or not.

But wait, aren't we supposed to pre-qualify or pre-judge our prospects?

Absolutely not! Let's not make assumptions about people based on their occupation, income, or any other external factor.

Consider the example of Joanne. She sells expensive health supplements. She might assume her lawn maintenance worker can't afford her supplements and withholds the offer.

But what if that worker actually values his health more than his financial situation and wants to invest in health supplements? What if the lawn maintenance worker thought, "Wow. I need these health supplements. If I get sick for just one day, I will lose hundreds of dollars."

If Joanne withheld gifting the option to buy her health supplements, that would be terrible.

Of course, her lawn maintenance worker could have also said, "Those health supplements are too expensive for me." But the point is that we should not pre-judge people. Let's allow them to have the option so they can make a decision for their lives.

It's not our place to judge, so let's offer the option and let them decide.

Prospects aren't dumb. They can figure out if our option makes sense for them now, or not.

Need some examples of a simple option?

Do our prospects want:

- more money in their lives, or less money
- to live longer, or to die quickly
- to reduce the wrinkles, or to keep watching the wrinkles get deeper
- an extra check every week, or to keep trying to get by on one paycheck
- to continue paying a higher electricity rate, or a lower rate
- to live in a house with natural cleaners or chemical cleaners
- And this simple list of options can go on and on.

Prospects are not dumb, they can figure this out. They hear our wonderful option, and then decide if it will benefit them now or not.

And this takes seconds

Prospects can make an instant decision if our option sounds good … or not. Humans make instant decisions. It is how our brains are wired.

We decide in seconds if something is worth pursuing … or not. Done.

And if our option seems like it fits, our prospects will beg us for more details.

This is where the big decision happens. In the beginning. Not at the end of some long boring recitation of facts.

So what would hold our prospects back from our wonderful option?

Think about it.

Our wonderful option is better than our prospects keeping their lives the same. Yet, some prospects won't take our wonderful option.

Why?

Let's make a partial list.

#1. No money. They barely have enough money for food at the moment. This means they have to wait before they can take advantage of our option. This might be embarrassing for them to admit, so they will give us a phantom objection so they can save face.

#2. They don't believe our promises. We forgot to leave our hype and exaggeration behind. We couldn't put our sales agenda away. "Be an active listener (80% listener 20% talker—primarily asking the right questions). Remember what we're doing is about identifying and solving their problem, not pushing our benefits and agenda.

#3. They are afraid of change. The risk of change is greater than their desire for our option. This is why when we make our offers, we want to consider reducing the risk of change. Humans hate risk.

#4. Mother dropped them on their head. Now they have negative programs about everything. Nothing will work for them. They feel destined for failure and won't make an effort to change their future.

#5. They don't qualify or fit what we offer. Not every human likes to exercise. Not every human has a computer. Not every human has a pet. Not every human likes coffee or alcohol. Not every human has recognition as their highest priority. Not every human believes that vitamins are necessary. These prospects won't qualify for what we offer as an option for their lives.

#6. Our offer explanation was too confusing or unclear.

Ah. Now we have the big picture we were looking for.

We gift an option. Prospects can take advantage of our option, or not.

Done.

Sweep out our head trash in one quick thought

We remove our fear of rejection by changing our intention.

There is no chance of rejection. We offer an option. They decide if this option fits in with their lives now, or not. We are not in charge of their decisions. We didn't choose their spouse. We didn't choose their job. We didn't choose the model of the car they drive.

Our prospects are responsible for the decisions they make in their lives. We don't live their lives for them. We don't know what's going on behind the scenes in their lives, so they are the best qualified to decide if they want to take our option or not. When we accept that, our fear of rejection goes away.

Now we don't have to stand in front of a mirror, yelling, "I am one with the universe. I am invincible. Rejection won't defeat me! I have no feelings!"

Instead, we enjoy our careers. All we do is gift people an option that can improve their lives. Then we step back, and let them decide.

Maybe these sentences will help us

When making our offers to prospects, we can reinforce the feeling that we are making our offers an option. This assures us that our prospects won't feel a forced sales agenda from us.

Since prospects are reactive, all we need to do is choose simple sentences that make our prospects relax. Here are some ideas of what we could add when making our offers:

- This may or may not work for you.
- I don't know if this will work for you, but you can decide that.
- Something for you to consider in the future.
- This may or may not be your cup of tea.
- Only you know if this fits you or not.
- I know you explore options, so here is one more to add to your list.
- Only you can decide if this is something to move forward on or not.
- This may or may not be a priority for you, but something to add to your list of options.
- This is another direction you can add to your choices.
- Before I show you how this works, I need to tell you something important. It is okay to say no to this business, and keep your life the same. But, it is also okay to say yes, and change your life forever.
- It is okay to say no. I just didn't want to feel guilty that I didn't mention this to you.

- I have two offers for you today. #1, keep your life the same. Don't change anything. And #2? Here is our option to fix your problem. You know your situation much better than me. I will let you choose. And if you choose option #2, I will explain how it works.

These sentences relax our prospects, but the biggest benefit is for us. This helps us change our intention and agenda. This removes our biggest fear when talking to prospects, and makes prospecting easy.

Think "output" instead of "outcome" when gifting people with our option.

Why does this thinking work so well?

Because our minds are prediction machines

The main program in our minds is survival. To survive, we need to predict what's going to happen next to protect ourselves. So, our brains are constantly guessing what will happen in the near future.

Some examples?

When walking, we see a set of stairs ahead of us. We predict that we should lift our feet when we approach the stairs. If we predict wrong, our faces will hurt.

When we see ice cream, we predict a delicious treat. We don't fear putting ice cream in our mouths.

When the ice cream truck starts moving away from us slowly, just before we reach it, we accurately predict that we can run and catch up. Instant motivation to action.

Let's get ready to cross a busy street. We see a wall of speeding traffic coming toward us. Our minds predict, "If we cross now, we are going to die!" So what is our motivation? To stop. Easy. We don't need goals or affirmations to make the decision to wait for the traffic to pass.

If someone talks too slowly, we interrupt and finish their sentences for them. We feel we know where the conversation is going. Rude? Yes. But it is what we do as humans.

And, here is the big one

Before we give a sales presentation, our minds remember our past. In the past, we got rejected. That felt awful. So we project that chance of rejection into our near future. Now we have reason to procrastinate or even fear starting our presentation. No wonder motivation is so hard. Our minds predict the possibility of a bad experience.

But when our agenda is to give prospects the gift of one more option in their lives, we predict a pleasant outcome. We finish our task by gifting the option. We are not attached to the outcome.

Fear of prospecting and selling defeated!

By changing our expectations, we won't need motivation to overcome fear. There will be no fear to overcome.

Is this the secret to the secret of motivation?

Well, at the very least, it is one of the secrets for sure.

We don't have to change our self-image. We don't have to be more confident. We don't even have to intensify our "why" for doing this business.

Instead, all we need to do is change our intention and expectations. In this case, our intention and expectations are to gift an option that will enhance our prospects' lives. Once we present our gift, our mission is complete.

Our new option is almost always better than our prospects' current situations. Our prospects will want what we offer, if their circumstances will allow. They know what is going on in their lives.

Magic.

But ... but ... how will we know what option to gift our prospects?

Listen.

Listeners have a huge advantage over talkers. Talkers are so intent on delivering their pre-scripted presentation, they won't wait for their prospects to tell them what problems they want solved.

Introverts are great listeners. Polite people are great listeners. And even talkers can be great listeners by biting their tongues and letting their prospects talk.

The purpose of business is to solve our prospects' problems.

Of all the problems that our prospects have, some of these problems could be solved by what we offer. Common sense will help us select the correct option to gift to our prospects.

And here is one more bonus

When we remove our "I got to get you to buy" agenda, and replace it with "here is an option that might help you" agenda, our prospects react to our agenda. They now think, "Hey! You are not begging or manipulating me to buy. This must be good. You seem confident that your offer is so good, there is no need to hype and oversell. I hope I can take advantage of this offer."

Prospects react to our confidence. They will feel great about our offer.

Finally ...

Let's improve our skills when making offers to our prospects. We want to have great wording ... while making our offers simple to understand ... and memorable ... with some tension-breaking humor ... with a clear option ... that sell.

Yes, this will take time to master, but the payoff is worth it.

Great offers rock!

WHAT IS THE #3 FACTOR IN MAKING GREAT OFFERS?

This book is not about the audience or our personal head trash. This book is about making great offers. Now that we have addressed the audience and the head trash, let's learn how to make our offers appealing.

Q. So what is the #3 factor in making great offers?

Answer: The actual offer. The option we give to our prospects.

While there are many strategies and tactics, let's keep our focus on:

- Creating our offers.
- Positioning our offers.
- And how we describe our offers.

Time for some fun now. We finally can make our offer.

Our head trash is gone. If we make an offer now, make it an option, and present it to prospects who qualify ... then two things can happen.

> #1. Our prospects will say "no" to the option we gift to them. This doesn't mean we are bad. It only means the

option we offered was bad for them at this moment. (And yes, we can try again with a better option.)

#2. Our prospects will say "yes" to the option we gift to them. Done. And now we can be partners while going through the details.

Do we like things in easy-to-follow steps?

Then we will plan our offer carefully. We won't make up an offer and tell ourselves, "I have a good feeling about this offer." Let's save our feelings for our therapists.

For our prospects, we need an offer so good that they will feel silly for turning our offer down. We want to make our offer a "no-brainer", so our prospects can make their decisions fast.

Will we create a great offer on our first try?

No.

In the beginning, we will be underwhelming. Later, when we get better at making our offers, we will look back and cringe at our first attempts. This is normal as we get better the more we practice.

What steps should we take to start our offer-making skills? How about these:

Step #1: Understanding our audience. This is why listening to our prospects' problems makes so much sense.

Step #2: Create an option for our prospects that is better than their current situation.

Step #3: Present our option as a gift. They can use the gift or not. This removes our agenda and calms our prospects.

Common sense. No need to be complicated. Simple is better. Prospects like simple.No need to impress or use hype.

If our offer is better for our prospects than keeping their current situation, they will want it.

We don't have to have superstar persuasion skills. We don't want to manipulate or convince our prospects into doing something they don't want. We offer a better option. That's it!

If our offer is easy for prospects to understand, they can make an instant decision before we ever explain the details.

Really?

Yes. Before our presentation.

Instant offers. Instant decisions.

How fast do prospects make up their minds? Lightning fast. Our brains have many things to think about. We have to decide if this current thought deserves more time, or if we should move on to the next thought. So, when we present an offer, prospects will pre-judge it and pre-judge it harshly in seconds.

How about an easy example? Ready?

You are starved. Hungry, hungry, hungry. I call and say, "Hey, I just picked up a hot pizza and a chocolate cake at the bakery. Mind if I come over?"

Hmmm. A pretty good offer. You are hungry. You like pizza. You love chocolate cake. I am only minutes away. How fast can you make a decision?

You answer, "I will leave the front door open!"

You didn't need to know the ingredients of the cake. You didn't even ask what type of pizza I had. Did you want to know about the company founder of the pizzeria? Did you want to hear testimonials about the chocolate cake?

No!

The decision was instant.

I had a great offer to a qualified and starving prospect with a hunger problem. I didn't need any persuasion skills or magic words.

Offer. One-second decision. Done.

Oh.

And this is the power of making a great offer to prospects. They can decide instantly.

Why is this important?

Think about our new team members. Will they have instant, high-level network marketing and persuasion skills when they join? Of course not.

But we can give them immediate success if we equip them with powerful offers. Now they can experience some success while learning the skills of our profession.

Here are examples of simple offers, where prospects make decisions after only a few words.

- Eat cookies. Lose weight.
- Turn your body into a fat-burning machine.
- Remove wrinkles while you sleep.
- Never overpay your mobile phone bill again.
- Fire your boss, and be your own boss.
- Live longer instead of dying quickly.
- Stop commuting and work from home.
- Retire before your parents do, and at full pay.

- Help your parents retire when you do, so you can enjoy free vacations together.
- Have three-day weekends forever.
- Get an extra paycheck every Friday.
- Make our skin look like a teenager's, but without the acne.
- Lose 10 pounds in the next 14 days.
- Get paid when your neighbors turn on their lights.
- Keep your current electricity supplier, but let us send you a lower bill. Use the savings for tacos for the family.
- Instant natural energy in a capsule, for 1/10th the cost of a Starbucks.
- In the next 60 days you could lose 20 pounds of unwanted body fat, without joining a sweaty gym.

Only a few words to make a decision? Yes. Unsure? Then let's make it even fewer words. Ready?

- Sugar-free
- One calorie
- On sale
- Turbo
- Proven results
- Best-seller
- Best-value
- New arrival
- Instant savings

Did we feel it?

How fast did our minds make a "yes" or "no" decision?

Fast, right? We know if this is something we want or not.

Yikes. This brings up an uncomfortable reality.

"The first few words or sentences of our offer could be 95% of our success!"

If our offer solves our prospects' problems and fixes our prospects' pain, their decision is easy.

We don't have to be a bargain.

We don't have to be the lowest price with the best terms.

Yes, prospects want a deal.

Yes, prospects want value.

But most of all, prospects want to stop the pain of their problems!

Instant decisions, but could we stretch our mindset further?

Consider the possibility that making an offer is better than leads.

Salesmen beg and scream for high-quality leads that are pre-sold. They want pre-screened, stress-free prospects so they can read a brochure to them. Well, that is a salesman's fantasy, but not reality. These salespeople don't even want to invest in the work of building rapport and trust.

But what if for a moment we forget about leads? We forget about targeting. We forget about funnels.

Instead, we consider a different way.

What if we offered a simple option to everyone in seconds? What would happen?

First, prospects react to getting an option instead of being sold through a sales presentation.

They think, "Let me hear the option to see if it would serve me or not. The only way an option can benefit me is if I take it. Let me look for positive ways that this option will work."

Now they are looking for "reasons why" our offer can work for them.

Prospects continue thinking. "Because this is an option, you are giving me the power to see if it fits my life now or not. I am in control of the decision. I won't feel manipulated by some persuasive sales technique by you. No need to be defensive."

Now we prevent rejection. This feels so good.

Our simple offer takes seconds.

This way is faster than pre-qualifying a lead

All we do is gift an option, an option that is better than our prospects' current situation. We allow our intelligent prospects to choose what is best for them at this time in their lives.

Prospects are not dumb. They can choose between something that will improve their lives, or keep their lives the same.

Their thoughts might be:

- "Do I want more money in my life, or less money?"
- "Do I want to lose weight one time and keep it off forever?"
- "Do I want to keep my wrinkles or get rid of them?"
- "I can do math. A lower bill is better than a bigger monthly bill."

- "Does retiring early feel better than working to age 80?"
- "Work from home or continue to fight an hour of traffic every morning?"

Our simple offer could take seconds, and it's faster than pre-qualifying a lead.

We gift an option that's better than what our prospects currently have, and let them choose what's best for them at this time in their lives.

Prospects aren't dumb. They can choose between something that will improve their lives or they can keep their problems.

"But my product is so boring. I can only think of one or two short offers."

Really?

Or are we being lazy and unimaginative?

Take any product or service and start collecting ideas now. Once we know that we are looking for fast and easy ways to make an offer, we will notice these gems in the future. Need an example?

A skincare and cosmetic networker asked for a few starter offers. Here were some of our initial suggestions to her.

- "Makes your skin look so good, you will never have to wear makeup again."
- "Avoid the Clown School of Makeup by using our coordinated color palettes."
- "Cheap makeup makes us look ... cheap."
- "Skin like a baby in only 14 days."
- "Feels so good that you can't stop touching your skin."

- "We call this the 'pore-reducer.'"
- "Makes your skin look so young that you won't be able to buy alcohol anymore."
- "Acne-buster!"
- "Stop laying in bed at night listening to your skin wrinkle."
- "Keep wrinkles away an extra 15 years."
- "Wrinkle-shrinker."
- "Lipstick that stays on your lips, not on cups and clothing."
- "Have natural long lashes, without gluing them on."
- "Makes your skin younger every night while you sleep."
- "Double-chin remover."
- "Lose those wrinkles!"
- "You never want your face to look older than you are."
- "Facelift in a bottle."
- "We don't want to look like a prune."
- "Get rid of the 'tech-neck' from looking at your phone all the time."
- "Have that spa look in just 12 minutes."

And these were only a start!

Yes, we can expand our offerings if we try.

One of my favorite single-panel cartoons is of a doctor talking to his fat businessman patient. The doctor offers:

"What fits your busy schedule better? Exercising one hour a day or being dead 24 hours a day?"

What if we don't believe that prospects make quick decisions?

Then, we will be like John, the fact-driven network marketer. Here is his conversation with his prospects.

John bores his prospects. "B-o-n-u-s … n-u-m-b-e-r … s-e-v-e-n …"

His presentation couldn't go any slower. Painful. And now his prospects start to twitch. Something bad is going to happen.

"We have to interrupt you, John. Don't go any further. We don't want to waste your time. We are not interested. This is not for us." John's prospects are in full eye-roll mode.

"But … but … how can you not be interested as you haven't seen the whole picture yet?" John pleads to talk more.

But his prospects respond, "We have to get off this call now. We … uh … have a pressing appointment we must get to."

We understand the cause of this scenario now.

Okay, but how about some clear examples

Our opening offer:

- "I can help your utility bill be larger or smaller, which one would you like me to do?"
- "I can help you be healthier and live longer, or help make your life shorter. Which one would you like me to talk about?"
- "I can help your bank account get larger, or help it get smaller. Which one would you like to talk about?"
- "I can help your skin look older … or younger. Which one is more interesting to you?"

Getting this initial "yes" decision is a start

Of course, we will have to do more. But if we start with our prospects having an open mind, and wanting our solution, the rest of our conversation gets easy. Our prospects are on our side, wanting what we offer.

Our job is to construct a creative offer that is a better option for our prospects' lives.

But ... but ... what if we don't feel creative?

Some people have natural creativity in their genes. Congratulations to them!

Us? Maybe not.

We think, "They didn't teach me creativity in school. Probably because it was too much work to grade creativity tests. It will take me forever to train my mind to be creative!"

The good news is that we don't have to have these exceptional creativity skills to make awesome offers. Then what do we need?

A checklist of basic tools

Each tool will prompt us to make small changes to our original boring offers. These tools help us look at new ways to improve our offers.

We don't have to use all of these basic tools, but it is nice to look at our offers through each tool's lens. We will see new possibilities from our new viewpoint.

And don't worry. Yes, there are a lot of tools we could learn, but the reality? We will only need a few of these most basic tools to improve.

Let's start looking at some of these building block tools now.

TOOL #1:
THE "OFFER SECRET"
SALESPEOPLE FORGET

The secret?

The "removal of risk" is more important than the "benefits of our offer."

Why?

Because humans want to remove all risks from their lives. Of course, this is not possible. But, the less risk our offer presents to our prospects, the more open-minded they will be.

So, how easy do we want to make it for our prospects to buy?

Let's review an old story that shows us the power of making our offers risk-free.

The farmer buys a horse

An old farmer wants to buy a horse for his farm. His internet search finds three horses for sale. He calls the salesperson and sets an appointment.

The first salesman arrives with a horse and makes the following offer.

"This horse is awesome. It has a full medical check-up. A super genetic lineage. It eats very little and will work all day. You can't go wrong. Give me money, and I will sell you this horse."

The farmer thinks, "What if this horse dies tomorrow, or what if this horse doesn't work out? I will lose my money."

The farmer tells the salesman, "I will get back to you."

The second salesman arrives with a horse and makes the following offer.

"This fully-trained horse will be perfect for you. And, I have testimonials from other farmers about how much they love the horses they bought from me. But to make this offer risk-free, give me your money, I will sell you this horse, and I will give you a 30-day money-back guarantee."

Again the farmer hesitates and thinks, "What if this horse dies tomorrow, or what if this horse doesn't work out? When I ask for my money back, will this salesman honor his guarantee? What if he doesn't? Then I will lose my money."

The farmer tells the salesman, "I will get back to you."

Finally, the third salesman arrives with a horse and makes the following offer.

"This horse will be perfect for you. But don't take my word on it. See for yourself. I will give you this horse now to try. In 30 days I will return. Then, you can give the horse back to me, or decide to keep the horse and pay me."

Now ... which salesman made the sale?

The answer is obvious.

When the third salesman returns after 30 days, the farmer greets him with a smile and says, "I'm keeping the horse. It has been great for my farm."

The first salesman had great features and benefits.

The second salesman had testimonials and social proof.

But what is stronger than features, benefits, and social proof?

Removing risk!

The more we eliminate risk, the more attractive our offer is to our prospects.

What are some extreme examples of removing or reducing the risk in our network marketing offers? Let's stretch our thinking. Remember, we don't have to go this far, but we want to know the potential power we could use when making offers to our prospects.

Example #1.

Let's start small. Can we offer a free sample of our product and come back later to take an order? Zero risk for our prospects. And prospects expect us to come back for the decision. Our chances are good that our prospects will give the product a fair trial.

But what if we sell services? Could we offer a free short-term trial and only bill them after the trial? Or, if we are confident, we can pre-pay for a week of the service.

Example #2.

We give our prospects a one-month supply of our products. We tell them, "I will come back at the end of 30 days. You can pay me for the products then, choose to re-order, or just give me the empty containers back. I only want you to become a customer after you've experienced these wonderful products and totally love them."

A bit more aggressive and risky for us, but we removed more risk from our skeptical prospects.

But what if we sell services? We could say this, "I will pre-pay your service bill for a month. In 30 days I will return. You can tell me what you want to do. You can reimburse me then for the one month's service if you love it, or we can cancel your service. Zero risk for you."

We won't want to offer this to every prospect. Having some business discernment is important. But, for our mother who doesn't believe us, this would be great. Or, for that influencer who will tell others, this could be the perfect advertising budget.

Example #3.

We say to our business prospect, "The startup kit is $500 and includes over $700 in products. I will pre-pay for the startup kit. Then, you and I will work over the next 30 days to sell this product. You can see for yourself how much others want it. We will use these sales to pay for your starter kit. So, between the sales of the product, and any bonuses that you earn during the first 30 days, we will pay for your startup costs. And if we don't earn the full amount back, you have a choice. Pay me back the difference, and keep all the extra products that we didn't sell yet. You know you will be getting repeat orders in the coming months. Or, you can give me back your startup kit and the unsold products."

But what if we sell services? We could say this, "I will pre-pay for your startup fees of $500. We will work together for 30 days. At the end of 30 days, you will know if this business is for you or not. If we earn more than $500, you will already be in profit. If we earn less than $500, you can walk away if you choose. I will take the loss on the difference. So, you know I will be working hard as your partner to help you succeed."

Do we have to go this far?

Of course not. These examples simply illustrate how removing risk will make our offers irresistible. Each of us has different comfort zones and risk tolerances.

Removal of risk is a huge lesson for us when making offers. The cloud of risk hangs heavy on our prospects' minds throughout our conversation. Let's acknowledge this potential sales killer.

And if we need to pull out all stops, to pull that ultimate lever, this is a good tactic.

How does this sound in real life? With cautious prospects?

Our prospect resists, "No, I don't want to join your part-time business. I don't want to take the risk. What if I join and fail?"

Ouch. Our prospect needs a part-time income. His retirement is in five years, and he has no savings. We feel this was his only chance.

We take a deep breath. "If you continue with your current job, and have no side income, you are guaranteed to retire ... broke. You won't have the extra money you need to cover your mortgage or your car payment."

"But, I don't wanna take the risk. I don't want to fail." Our prospect doesn't like the reality.

We continue. "We hate risk also. Nobody likes risk. When we take a risk, we can win or lose. Nothing is guaranteed. But, if you don't start a part-time business, your failure is guaranteed. There is a 100% chance of failure if you don't try. Yes, starting the part-time business is a risk, but it is better than guaranteed failure."

Our prospect thinks for a moment and decides to join. Having "a chance" feels better than having no chance at all.

Risk is a part of life. The only guarantee in life is that if we don't try, we will fail.

So which offer feels better?

Option 1: Having a 100% chance of failure?

Option 2: Taking a risk and having a chance to change our lives?

Most prospects will take our offer of "having a chance." Few will choose the 100% guaranteed failure option.

When we make clear, easy-to-understand offers, it makes it easy for our prospects to make their final decisions.

Let's give others a chance. Let's make clear and compelling offers.

But what else can we do to remove risk?

Let's use our imagination. Could we:

- Arrange low and affordable payments?
- Offer more satisfied testimonials?
- Extended warranties?
- Take our prospects to visit satisfied customers?
- Promise to work with them until they get a certain result?

Let's put ourselves in our prospects' shoes. They want certainty, not risk.

But this is only one tool we can use to help our prospects make decisions. Let's discover more.

RISK PARALYZES OUR PROSPECTS

We know that our products and services are the best on the market. Our prospects would be fools to refuse our wonderful offers.

The reality?

Even if our products are beyond awesome, our prospects resist buying from us.

Why? What are they thinking? Don't they want what is better for them? Don't they want a better life?

So why does risk dominate our prospects' thinking?

The number one program in our subconscious minds is survival. Humans want to avoid risk. If we make a risky mistake, well, that could be our end. Not good. We have a natural resistance to change. Any change invites risk. It will take a compelling offer for us to take on more risks in our lives.

A quick example?

I am at home, watching my favorite television show. My sofa is safe and comfortable. No need to move. No motivation to move. And, why should I risk pulling a hamstring by going outside for a healthy walk?

I will need a very compelling offer to convince me that trying to change my situation is worth the risk.

The compelling offer?

Donuts.

I can smell the aroma of fresh donuts from the shop next door.

The taste and dopamine release from power eating a dozen donuts far outweighs the risk of a possible hamstring injury by walking next door. The rewards are great. I know that eating a dozen donuts will deliver the feeling I want. I have previous donut trips to prove this.

The risk? Very small. I only have to take a few steps. No one will criticize me. After all, who could criticize anyone in their quest for donuts? This is a worthy cause.

We need to show our prospects that the benefits of our products outweigh the risks. We need to prove to them that they will thrive with our products, not just survive.

This summarizes a compelling offer.

Part #1: A great reward.

Part #2: Low risk.

When we are new in sales, we concentrate on our products' facts, features, and benefits. We have charts, PowerPoint presentations, videos, and glowing testimonials. We create a picture of tremendous rewards for our prospects.

But, we neglect to address the low-risk factor. We forget to show our prospects how their decision will feel safe to them. So then, they hesitate. They hold back. That nagging risk in the back of their minds prevents them from taking action.

One definition of selling is the "removal of risk" from our prospects.

We are not only selling our benefits, but also the assurance that their decision won't end badly. That they will come out ahead.

When our prospects feel secure, they take action. Isn't that what we want our prospects to do?

There are two big risks.

First, the common risk. The loss of money when prospects don't enjoy their purchase. This is why companies provide money-back guarantees. But if money-back guarantees were enough, wouldn't every prospect buy?

Whoops! They don't. There must be another risk holding them back. This is the hidden risk that new salespeople forget to address. What is that second risk?

The social risk.

How will our prospects feel if their purchases don't work out? Our prospects might think, "I am a loser. I made a poor decision. Why did I attempt to make my life better instead of staying where I am? I hate this feeling."

But, it gets worse. Our prospects' negative thoughts continue. "What will others think of me? They will see my mistake and make fun of me. I hate feeling humiliated for stupid things in front of others."

This social risk is the biggest risk. This is the secret risk that holds prospects back.

We must assure them that no one will make fun of their decision. We must assure them that they won't be the butt of jokes for making this decision.

Then, how do we reduce that social risk in our prospects' minds?

1. We do this by positioning ourselves not as a salesperson, but as a guide. We are here to help them make the best decision for their lives. And if things don't work out, we have their back with support and solutions.

2. Remind our prospects of good decisions they made in the past. They took a risk to learn to drive, when they got married, and tried the food at their new and now most favorite restaurant. Our prospects love to listen when we recognize their past good decisions.

3. Testimonials are great, but we can make them better. Stories and quotes from other people lend credence to what we say. We can talk about how some of these testimonials were skeptical in the beginning. Then, how much they appreciate the good decision they made. Remember, everyone wants a better life.

4. Use statistics. Prospects default to, "Numbers don't lie." There seems to be safety in numbers as proof.

5. What risks do our prospects take by not buying from us? Yes, not buying from us could cause an even bigger risk to our prospects. Some examples?

   - If we sell vitamins, not taking vitamins could put junk food eaters at more risk.

- If we sold a part-time business, not having a second income, and having 100% of their income at risk with only one job, could be a serious risk.

- If we sold a long-term utility contract, not taking advantage of the contract could risk increased rates for our prospects in the future.

Not taking advantage of what we offer could look like a major blunder to their friends.

Social risk runs deeper than a simple monetary loss. Our survival programs want us to have good standing with our peers. We don't want to risk "losing face" over a bad decision.

As professionals, let's not limit our selling to the facts, features, and benefits of our products. Yes, sell the rewards, but let's not forget that removing risks is more important to our prospects.

A good offer is not about getting money for what we offer. It is about removing the fear of change from our prospects' minds.

TOOL #2:
IF WE CAN'T CHANGE OUR OFFER, CAN WE CHANGE OUR POSITIONING?

Humans make decisions instantly, based on no information.

PowerPoint presenters hate this. They are like crack addicts adding more slides, more information, more data, and more charts. That was the reality in the 1990s, but we know better now.

We make decisions on our emotions, not from facts and figures. These emotions come from the current programs in our subconscious minds.

Our subconscious minds don't use words. Instead, they signal our decision in less than a second through feelings. We often hear people describe this as a "gut feeling" or instant "like" or "dislike."

Here is a quick example and then a solution

I tell this story often.

A distant relative asks us, "Can I take your children skydiving with me?"

Now depending on what our children did to us while they were growing up, we would think, "Oh no. Please don't take my babies skydiving!" or "I would help push them out of the plane!"

Assuming we love our children, our immediate answer would be, "No!"

How long did it take us to make that decision? It was instant. We have an internal program called "love of family." This emotion triggers an instant decision.

Isn't it interesting that we made our final decision before our distant relative even started his skydiving presentation? Before he told us that he was a professional skydiver? Before he told us that he was successful three out of four times? Before he told us that we are only going to skydive one inch?

Yes, we make decisions before the details and presentation. We feel that instant decision in less than a second.

Uh-oh.

If people make decisions instantly based upon their programs to our offers, then … what can we do if their programs tell them "no" to our offers?

Hmmm.

What if we can't change what we offer?

Our network marketing company supplies the product or service we market to our prospects. We probably can't control the product, service, or even the pricing.

Well, we can hold our breath and wait for the company to improve the product. We can complain our product is too hard to sell. Then, maybe in a couple of years, we can resume marketing our business when they finally improve the product.

This sounds silly, but many networkers say, "I need the company to change this before I get started." These people belong to the "Just One More Thing" club of procrastinators.

Yuck!

Waiting for something to change is not a good plan.

What else can we do?

If we can't change our product, or can't change our offer, then what?

Change the "positioning" of our offer in our prospects' minds

We can change how we describe our offers. Our new description could resonate with different programs in our prospects' minds.

How our prospects perceive our product offer can make a difference.

Prospects compare our products to other products.

They compare our products to other solutions.

They judge how likely our product will fix their problem.

They think about how our product might make a difference, and ... our positioning possibilities are endless.

Let's re-describe the skydiving offer

Same product. But let's allow our prospects to see our product from a different point of view.

Remember, we only asked the parents to allow their children to jump one inch. But, we didn't get to describe this one-inch jump because as parents, we had already made up our minds. Our mistake.

Let's re-describe this offer now.

"Can I take your children on a fun adventure? We are going to dress up and pretend to be skydivers and we will jump one inch."

As parents, we think, "One inch! That seems safe. I bet they would enjoy that pretend adventure."

See how our new description goes to a different program in the parents' minds?

Our offer now is to jump one inch.

In the first example, the human mind made a decision before we even got to our one-inch description. That was a bad positioning or description of our offer. This is how bad our offers sounded in the past. We didn't realize what we were doing.

In the second example, we redefined our offer in a way that agreed with a different program in the parents' minds.

Same offer, but two different results

We may not be able to change our offers, but we can often change the way we present our offers to others. And if we change or reframe our offers, we might change their instant decision from "no" to "yes."

How powerful can a little change in positioning be?

Let's talk ice cream.

Everyone wants healthy, low-sugar, cream-free, chemical-free, organic ice cream that builds muscle. That is not going to happen. We know there are chemicals in our favorite desserts.

So why not do a little positioning? It only costs a few words.

This ice cream shop advertises 100% Magical Ingredients!

Magical? That was enough to get me to buy. I could suspend my logical defenses long enough to make the purchase and enjoy this treat.

Simple positioning at work.

Positioning matters

Take a crowded market such as nail polish.

How many types of nail polish are there? How many different prices? How many nail polishes have different ingredients?

It is hard to stand out … unless we use some positioning.

Many years ago, I saw this ad.

Brilliant positioning.

Chantilly Peach covers unsightly toenails which make your feet look smaller which make your shoes look sexier which make your legs look longer which make your butt look better which means you can have another slice of cheesecake.

Yes, this nail polish is different. They positioned their nail polish away from their competitors, and well, they created a niche of their own.

Now, let's try another product. Ready?

The Nasty Diet Protein Powder product

How do our prospects look at our product? They report, "This is a lousy-tasting powder that makes disgusting protein shakes. Its chalky texture induces gagging and leaves a terrible aftertaste. You have over 1,000 other competitors selling lousy-tasting powder mixes too. Nothing special here. Let's move on. We have donuts to eat."

Now, we can't change the product, but we can change the positioning. Here is how we will do it.

We ask ourselves, "What problem are these prospects trying to solve? What do they want to accomplish?"

Hmmm.

Well, they are still fat. So hard-core, serious weight loss may not be their primary driver here.

What they want is a diet program that is fun and easy to do. And even if they don't lose weight, they will feel good because they can tell themselves, "I tried."

Now, based on what they want, let's make a new offer that will better position our Nasty Diet Protein Powder in their minds. Ready?

We offer free membership in our diet club at the local community center. Members come every Wednesday morning at 11:45 AM. They socialize and compare dessert recipes. We demonstrate what an exercise would look like if they saw one. Next, we tell them that they all look thinner.

Finally, we break for the potluck luncheon where every member brought their favorite desserts. Our members love our diet club. The only requirement for them to participate is to purchase a can of Nasty Diet Protein Powder to decorate their kitchen shelves.

But what about a service? Can we reposition how our prospects see our service?

Identity theft protection

Is there competition? Yes.

But we could position our offer not against the cheaper competition, but against an inevitable problem. How?

With this simple statement:

"Criminals have your credit card and passwords already. They just haven't got to it yet."

This will change our prospects' thinking from comparison shopping … to having an impending problem, and they feel confident that we can fix it.

Positioning matters.

A 9% discount?

Ask any professional shopper, "How would you feel if you got a 9% discount at the mall?"

They will laugh until their eyeballs hurt.

They won't even consider going into a mall store unless it has a sign offering a minimum of 70% discount. A 9% sale is ridiculous.

Enter positioning.

Here is how one shopping mall convinces hard-core shoppers to flock to their mall on a special day every year.

They announce weeks in advance that every store in their mall won't charge sales tax on this upcoming special day. The shoppers can't wait. No sales tax!

What happens?

On that "no sales tax" day shoppers flood the mall in a shopping frenzy. They have a great time. They anticipated this special day for weeks.

But sales tax is only 9% … hmmm.

A 9% off sale at the mall doesn't sound interesting. But a simple re-positioning puts this one-day event into a different space in the shoppers' minds. They look forward to this special day every year.

"But I want to earn big money or I won't even try!"

Our prospect complains that unless he can earn big money quickly, why even try? "I earn $1,000 a week now. I won't spend time building your tiny business. It will take too long to build it to $1,000 a week."

Time for some re-positioning.

Our prospect earns $200 every day. So earning an extra $200 a week could mean there is no need to come into the regular job on Fridays. Yes, an extra $200 a week could mean:

"Three-day weekends forever!"

Re-positioning at its finest

My friend, Tom Paredes, used to be an army recruiter. His first days attempting to recruit high school students showed no results. What was his original offer to join the army?

"It's like going back to primary school. You will get yelled at by mean instructors, you'll have no freedom, and all you can think about is how to escape from boot camp. We're talking institutional food here. Basic calories, no taste. Dress code? Heavy combat boots and dull, ill-fitting uniforms. If you live through your boot camp experience you can graduate to become a moving target for enemy sharpshooters. Oh yeah, did I mention the pay? You'll receive the absolute minimum allowed by law."

Not very enticing, is it?

Tom re-positioned his offer and added a little romance. This is how he successfully presented the Army opportunity.

"Do you want fun, travel, and adventure? The Army will give you all that and more. In fact, they'll even pay you while you are having the time of your life. Think about it. You can travel to exotic places all over the world. And, you won't have to pay a single airline fare or hotel bill. The Army appreciates your participation so much that they even provide you with all your clothing needs with their unique designer fashions. Forget about those high clothing prices downtown. Never pay another health club membership fee again. You'll look forward to supervised exercise instruction with a highly qualified personal trainer. You'll enjoy long nature walks and even your meals will be provided. Do you want even more excitement? The Army will place live ammunition in your hands as you celebrate your good fortune with fellow club members. And, as I said before, not only will the Army cover all your expenses, they'll even pay you money to ensure that you are having the time of your life!"

Tom became a top recruiter by repositioning the offer.

Repositioning works for everything when you use a little imagination

A distributor sold a nutritional drink with ketones. He said, "I showed our brochure to my prospects, and they didn't buy. Why?"

The brochure had one general message directed at prospects of many different backgrounds. As professional network marketers, we can reposition the message for our prospects. That is why our companies need us. If a brochure or video did all the selling, companies could save a lot of money by not paying us.

So how could we customize the ketone message for our prospects' needs?

Offer #1 to a college student. "Our brains use ketones. When do you think would be a good time to flood your brain with ketones?"

Offer #2 to a lazy dieter: "You can starve yourself for three days to get into ketosis so your body produces ketones, or you could drink this for immediate ketones."

Offer #3 to a workout enthusiast: "Get ketones in 59 minutes to amplify your workouts."

Offer #4 to a health enthusiast: "We know ketones are great for our bodies and our brains. Now you can drink instant ketones."

We could keep going on and on, but here is the key.

If we approach a prospect and the prospect says "no"... our prospect may not be saying "no" to our offer, but only to how we described our offer.

Different prospects have different motivations.

Positioning matters

Prospects compare. That is the easiest way for their brains to work.

50+ years ago, a hair spray product aired a commercial for their product.

Two Chinese ping pong experts were in a high-speed match. One player's hair flew everywhere with each strike. The other player? Perfect hair that didn't move one tiny bit.

Yes, the hair spray product worked wonders compared to … nothing!

But the buyers didn't care. They wanted hair that didn't move and this product became a best-seller.

The positioning wasn't against competing products. The positioning was against nothing.

Sometimes we don't have to change what we offer. Simply changing what's in our prospects' minds will create big results.

TOOL #3: EMOTION

How would it feel to never fear objections?

Really. Take a deep breath. Pause.

Can you imagine that feeling right now?

Or, how would it feel to have eager prospects waiting for your offer? Wouldn't that be great?

What we are experiencing is our emotional response to these questions.

Logic is great, but emotions cause humans to take action. Without emotion, our offers fall flat. They might sound nice, but no one will take action.

We only have moments to impress our prospects, so we want to activate their emotions as soon as possible.

Only moments to impress our prospects? Is that the reality?

Yes.

The Olympic thumb of my sister-in-law

I saw my sister-in-law scroll through a social media video website at warp speed. It was a blur. Her left hand held her cup of coffee. Her eyes and attention seem to be on a television program. But her right thumb? It was scrolling through the video thumbnails on her smartphone, non-stop. She did this so fast that her right thumb formed a small breeze. Truly a remarkable dexterity feat.

Think about the creators of those videos. They spent hours planning, editing, and uploading their masterpieces. Their reward? Nothing. They were only a microsecond of pixels flashing by the phone screen my sister-in-law wasn't even watching. Sad to see the wasted efforts of these video creators.

This is our fate if we can't slow down our prospects' attention. No one will hear or consume our message.

How we listen to salespeople.

A salesman interrupts and demands our attention. Think of how fast our thoughts change. In a few seconds, our thoughts could be:

- What is this salesman trying to sell me?
- I don't want to spend any money. I have lottery tickets to buy.
- It looks like he missed a spot when he shaved.
- That sounds like someone coming to the front door.
- Oh, look! There is a squirrel.
- I wonder how long this is going to last.
- Why is my neck itching?
- All sales pitches are too good to be true.
- I think my mother-in-law dyes her hair.

This is a dead end. So, let's move on to the solution.

Four little words!

We need a solution. Why?

Because when we talk, most people don't listen. If they don't hear our words or offer, we have no chance.

In a flash, our human thoughts drift to:

- I am so starved. I could eat a giant pizza.
- Did I forget my dentist appointment this morning?
- Why do I always misplace my car keys?
- Do I have to renew my driver's license soon?
- Be careful of scams. So many scams.
- I think I will binge-watch my favorite show tonight.

Our minds are like having 1,000 television channels running at the same time. Thoughts enter our minds and then exit in microseconds. Some thoughts don't even get into our minds. We push out most thoughts with a new thought. And, we do this over and over again.

This constant mind chatter is noise in the background. We don't pay attention to it. We are too busy moving on to the next new thought.

Do any thoughts ever get through? Well, if a thought does get through, here is what happens.

We hear parts of that thought in our minds. Then, we filter out words, add personal biases, think about other experiences, and of course, that means we are onto a different thought.

If this happens to us, it happens to our prospects. When we talk, our prospects will only hear a few passing words unless we take action to slow down this hyper mental activity. This is not miscommunication. This is no communication. Not good if we want to get our message into our prospects' minds.

We need to get their attention and then keep it focused on us and what we offer.

"How would it feel ..." Four little words with giant consequences

When we say these four little words, we affect our prospects' brains.

Do we remember the beginning of this chapter? Probably not. But if we did, here is what happened. This chapter started with the four little magic words: "How would it feel ..."

Then, we continued with these four questions:

- How would it feel to never fear objections?
- Really, can you imagine that feeling right now?
- Or, how would it feel to have eager prospects waiting for your offer?
- Wouldn't that be great?

The four little words, "How would it feel," stimulate the brains of our prospects. Why?

Secret #1. We start with a question

Uh-oh. A question? That means our prospects must stop their minds from wandering, and then think about our question. The human mind can entertain one thought at a time. We want to make sure it is our thought that is occupying their minds.

Questions force our prospects to slow down and think of their answer. They think, "So, how would I feel if this equipment saved me an hour every day? I would feel great. I could take off work early. Beat the traffic. And have an extra hour with the family."

When we hear a question, we must stop and think about that question. Then, we must come up with our answer. This is a great way to keep our message longer inside of our prospects' minds.

Notice how the "how would it feel ...?" creates a great open-ended question? This helps our prospects think longer as they can't answer open-ended questions with a simple "yes" or "no" reply.

Want to feel how our brains immediately search for an answer to the question? What if we heard this question?

"How would it feel if our company announced an extra week of holiday every year?" Can we picture our feelings?

This brings us to the second secret.

Secret #2: Movie time!

We say, "How would it feel?" Our prospects create a movie in their minds of something good or bad happening to them in the future. Our minds are very visual. We create movies inside of our minds. We don't think in words. We think in pictures. And most times we think in movies. Movies rock!

In a way, we can control the movies in our prospects' minds. We can have them think of a happy ending or a painful and uncomfortable future experience.

Movies feel real to our brains. Can we remember sitting in a movie theater and feeling like we are part of that movie? We jumped when the hero gets surprised. We feel pain when the villain hurts someone.

The better we design our question, the more our prospects will feel like they are in that movie. Need an example?

"How would it feel to wake up every morning before the alarm clock, but to have so much energy that you can't wait to grab a cup of coffee and jog with the dog?"

Do we see the mini-movie inside of our heads?

Secret #3: Prospects answer in their own words

Computer programmers talk to their minds in different words than poets. We each have our unique vocabulary and phrasing of how we talk to ourselves. We talk to ourselves non-stop every day of our lives.

This is a problem for salespeople. We talk to people in a way that we talk to our minds. We have our industry terms and jargon that may mean different things to our prospects. This makes our message a little fuzzy and unclear.

When our prospects answer our questions, they use their words and vocabulary. They think in their own words, not ours. So when we can use their words, our message is loud and clear. Yes, we could be talking about the same offer, but we will see that offer in different ways based on how we talk to ourselves.

In the previous chapter, we talked about an America shopping mall. Most purchases have a 9% or a 10% sales tax added on at the point of sale. Once a year, the local shopping mall has a big sales day. They announce, "No sales tax tomorrow! Free sales tax day!"

What happens? People pack the mall, wall-to-wall, with excited shoppers buying everything in sight. It is a mob. The shopping mall's management tested and knows what is the exact language of the local shoppers. ("No sales tax tomorrow! Free sales tax day!")

Now, the local shopping mall could have announced this: "All stores. 9% discount tomorrow."

We know the results. No one is going to get into their car for a 9% off sale. The mall is already littered with 20% to 40% off sales that shoppers ignore. This is the wrong language.

When shoppers think of a free sales tax day, they get excited. When they think of a 9% off sale, they fall asleep.

Years ago, the shopping mall manager was a good listener. She listened to the exact words the shoppers used, and created the free sales tax day promotion. She deserves a raise.

So, how would it feel to pay no sales tax over the next 24 hours? Great!

Secret #4: Prospects will sell themselves

Who is the better salesperson?

1. Us, with our wonderful message? Or,
2. Our prospects when they sell themselves with their own words?

No contest. Our prospects win every time.

Our prospects will believe what they tell themselves more than what we tell them.

All we need to do is ask, "How would it feel ...?" Then, take a deep breath. Wait while our prospects slow down to create their own sales movie inside of their heads. And finally, allow our prospects to see their future.

Their minds are opening up to the possibilities of what they could do with what we have to offer.

The best salespeople get out of the way and let their prospects sell themselves.

So, how would it feel to stand by silently, while our prospects sell themselves? Yeah, this is getting easier and easier.

Secret #5: "Feel"

We used the emotional word, "feel", in our question. We asked, "How would it feel ...?"

Now our prospects have to slow down their thinking even more.

First, they have to create the movie inside of their minds.

Second, they also have to notice their feelings.

Third, they must report back to us.

Our message and offers now take up residence in our prospects' minds. They hear what we say. They can't dismiss our words. This is a superpower.

Amateur salesmen rush through their features and benefits. This is a huge mistake. It isn't what we say that matters. It is what our prospects hear and think about that makes the difference. Let's give our prospects time to digest the wonderful things we present to them.

So, how would it feel if our prospects internalized our message, and thought longer about how our message can serve them?

Secret #6: "Emotions"

"Feel" is an emotion. How do prospects make decisions?

On facts? Or, on emotions?

Emotions, of course. With emotions we tap into the decision-making part of our prospects' brains. How good is that? This is where the action is.

If humans were honest, this would be the conversation.

Salesman: "How did you decide to buy?"

Prospects: "It was an emotional decision. That is how I make all of my decisions. That is the job of my subconscious mind. Now, give me a few rational and logical facts to back up my emotional decision, as I don't want to look bad to others."

We can't change the way humans make decisions. But, that is okay. Wants and emotions are great for decisions.

So, how would it feel to deliver our offer or message directly to our prospects' subconscious minds, where emotions make the final decisions?

The big difference?

"Needs" are rational facts and benefits. Our conscious minds deal with the rational.

"Wants" are more emotional, and reside in our decision-making subconscious minds. We are closer to the action. "Wants" are what we should be selling.

We can't change the way humans make decisions. And the good news is that we don't have to change. Instead, we can learn to present to the emotional wants of our prospects.

So, how would it feel to use these magic four words to help our prospects hear and understand what we offer?

Now, let's do some examples

For sales training:

- How would it feel to never fear objections?

- How would it feel to have rejection–free icebreakers to start conversations?
- How would it feel to be surrounded by other top salespeople at the convention?
- How would it feel to get prospects immediately on our side?
- How would it feel if our message got through every time?
- How would it feel to be the top salesperson in your company?

For financial products:

- How would it feel to retire early?
- How would it feel to have extra money for travel?
- How would it feel to send our kids to the best colleges?
- How would it feel to have zero credit card balances?
- How would it feel if you could buy your next car with cash?
- How would it feel if your mortgage payments were lower?

For a part-time business opportunity:

- How would it feel if you were your own boss?
- How would it feel to make an extra $500 per month?
- How would it feel to never have to ask for a raise again?
- How would it feel to fire your boss?
- How would it feel to be paid what you are worth?
- How would it feel to have two paychecks every month?

For diet products:

- How would it feel to lose weight by changing your breakfast?

- How would it feel to lose weight one time, and keep it off forever?
- How would it feel never to count calories ever again?
- How would it feel if you never had to worry about your weight?
- How would it feel if you could diet, but never feel hungry?
- How would it feel to lose 10 pounds before the end of the month?

For travel:

- How would it feel to take five-star holidays for the price of a Holiday Inn?
- How would it feel to get paid to travel the world?
- How would it feel if your job was to find the best travel deals?
- How would it feel if you never had to stand in line at the airport again?
- How would it feel if you could get free hotel rooms for your family and friends?
- How would it feel to take the children to Disney World instead of your mother-in-law's for their vacation?

For utilities and services:

- How would it feel if your mobile phone bill was lower?
- How would it feel if you got a huge discount on your electricity bill?
- How would it feel to have a home security system that cost you nothing?

- How would it feel to get paid for referrals to your current service providers?
- How would it feel to have blazing internet speed?
- How would it feel to get free upgrades on your cable and Internet service?

As we see, we can make these questions about almost anything, even skincare.

- How would it feel if acne were a thing of the past?
- How would it feel to get compliments on your skin all the time?
- How would it feel to have people ask you what skincare products you use?
- How would it feel to never have to worry about dry or flaky skin again?
- How would it feel to have healthier skin in only six days?
- How would it feel to have a natural skincare glow that doesn't require makeup?

But, could we say this instead?

"What would happen if ...?"

Yes, that works too, but our prospects will report what they see, not what they feel. They report facts or events.

Feelings are emotions.

Our subconscious decision-making mind works on emotions.

But, if you enjoy this alternate phrase, let's do a couple of examples.

- What would happen if you never had to show up for work again?
- What would happen if you could fire the boss and start your own business?
- What would happen if you could get all the tax deductions that big corporations get?
- What would happen if you earn more money part-time than your spouse did full-time?
- What would happen if you got an extra paycheck every Thursday?
- What would happen if you knew exactly what to say so that you would always be confident in the future?

Do you remember "Needs vs. Wants?"

Needs are logical.

We figure out our needs with our rational, intelligent conscious minds. That is the weak part of our minds that have no say in what we do.

Wants are emotional.

We don't NEED to eat that extra piece of cake. But we desperately WANT to eat that extra piece of cake to satisfy our subconscious minds.

None of us are immune from this thinking. For example, I love Mexican food.

The four basic ingredients of Mexican food? Fat, grease, lard, and salt. I certainly don't need Mexican food three times a day, but I want it. And no matter how hard and rational I am, a few … okay, quite a few Mexican meals slip into my weekly diet.

Our subconscious minds are powerful. They are the source of our emotions and feelings which drive us to action.

If it wasn't for the motivation of emotion and feelings, few people would get married.

Let's not discount the power of feelings.

The reality?

Humans make decisions based on what they "feel" is best, not on what they "think" is best.

When prospects have an emotional desire or a want, selling is effortless.

Look for prospects who desire what we offer for a stress-free selling career.

So ask ourselves, "How can I use questions to trigger more emotions from prospects in our offers?"

TOOL #4:
HOW BIG IS THAT
FIRST STEP?

My new personal trainer ascends from hell, brushing the dirt off his shoulders.

"Okay. Time for our first step. Let's warm up with 100 push-ups."

Push-ups?

If I could do a push-up, I wouldn't need a personal trainer. He doesn't appear to have a sense of humor. Just as well, as he just got fired.

Lesson learned.

When we make the first step too big,
our prospects hesitate

So what offer could a professional personal trainer make so that the first step for "chubby me" would be possible?

"Okay. Time for our first step. Let's warm up with a stretch. From your sitting position, slowly stretch to your right and reach into your gym bag and grab a donut."

Yeah! That would work. I'm "all in" and ready to sign a "personal trainer for life contract" … after I eat my donut.

The same is true for our network marketing prospects. When we make our offer and the first step appears achievable, our chances of success skyrocket. We need to make our prospects feel they can succeed.

If our prospects believe they can do the first step, they will assume the following steps are possible also. Their attention is on the very first step. Our prospects won't bother to think too far into the future.

Remember this old saying?

"A journey of 1,000 miles starts with a single step."

We want to sell our prospects on taking that first step. Then, with the momentum rolling, it will be easier for them to visualize the outcome. And as a bonus, if the first step appears easy, we will get fewer objections from our prospects.

How can we shrink that first step?

#1: Which is a better offer?

Results quickly … or results later?

That wasn't hard.

When we offer fast results it is easy for our prospects to want our offers. So what would prospects want as fast as possible?

- To break even or profit on their initial investment
- To fire their boss instead of suffering years in an undesirable job
- A way to earn bonuses now while waiting for the residual income to build

- A chance to earn enough now to replace one day at work every week

Can we emphasize the quick wins our prospects will get when they take our offers? Humans are naturally short-term thinkers. Now is always more powerful than later.

This is why 18-year-old prospects fail to get excited about long-term residual income and retiring ten years early.

We want to shrink the time to the first big payback our prospects will receive.

#2: How hard will this be?

If our revolutionary offer is complicated, difficult to understand, and hard to do, expect massive resistance. Prospects hesitate to volunteer for difficult tasks. They prefer the habits and processes they do now.

Examples of difficult offers?

- A structured fasting timetable with handfuls of tablets to take every day
- Complicated skincare regimes that take 30 minutes
- Services that require extra time
- Instructions that are hard to understand
- Efforts that will require leaving our comfort zones
- Learning new technologies

Prospects want ease and convenience, not challenges. Their lives are hard now and they don't want to make them harder.

#3: How big is my investment?

Time invested is time that we will never get back. On the plus side, if our offers give our prospects more time, this is a huge bonus in our favor. Everyone complains about not having enough time, and if we can help, we will be popular.

If we want to talk about the long journey to success, now may not be the right time. Our prospects haven't received any quick wins yet, so their confidence isn't high. No one wants to look forward to a long and painful journey.

Also, our prospects will think, "Is taking this first step worth the cost of changing my current life? This will cost me time and money, so I better be sure it is worth it."

#4. How big is my risk?

Humans hate risk. That is why Tool #1 is all about reducing risk.

What else can we do to make this first step easier and less risky?

- Offer a free trial or sample. This gives prospects a chance to try our product or service before they commit to buying it.
- Break down the offer into smaller steps. This will make it seem less daunting and more achievable.
- Or, how about a low-cost introductory offer?
- Make our offer clear and easy to understand. When we don't understand everything, we will have doubts in the back of our minds holding us back.

- Remind our prospects that their success is inevitable with our help.

#5: How much can I delay?

We think, "If I have to do it now, wow! I better be sure. But if I can delay some things to the future, that doesn't seem so bad. I'll worry about the future later."

Can we delay the full payment?

Can we extend the guarantee?

Can we give them a little more time before making the big investment?

#6: Focus the vision on the outcome.

Let's make our benefits and outcome larger so that their time and money investment feels worth it. This is a great time to pile on all those extra goodies we love to talk about. Yes, remind them of the recognition, the free trips, the feeling of accomplishment, the security of the extra money.

#7: Convenience and speed can be better than free.

We value our time and our efforts. So imagine a trip to the Universal Studios theme park. We spent a fortune on airline tickets and hotel expenses, and now we are in line to buy tickets.

The question is, "After our huge investment to get here, will we spend a few more dollars to get the premium tickets? Those special tickets that allow us to bypass the 45 minutes we would wait in line for each ride?"

Yes. We didn't spend thousands of dollars to bake in the hot sun waiting in long lines. Convenience and speed rock.

That is why dieters drink an expensive protein shake instead of the free option of walking two hours more every day.

And this is why spending a few hundred dollars to start a network marketing business is preferable to renting an office, hiring employees, arranging insurance, advertising, marketing, and all of the other expenses and headaches of another business.

The first step is the hardest

If we can shrink the first step, we make it easier for our prospects to want our offers.

What is the smallest possible first step that skeptical prospects could take? Once they have that first step successfully under their belt, the following steps will become easier. And as their confidence grows, their train will pick up speed and their vision of the future will grow bigger and brighter.

TOOL #5:
ULTIMATE BENEFITS
(TWO WORDS)

"It's not what we make … it's what we make happen."

We love what we offer so much that we forget about the ultimate benefits to our prospects. We have to remind ourselves of what is important to our prospects. If they don't see the value in what we are offering, they won't work with us.

It's too hard for our short attention span prospects to connect the dots. We can't expect them to figure out why our offer is important to them. They give up.

Enter the words "so that"

Let's add this simple phrase to our features and benefits list. Now our prospects experience an easy shortcut to see their ultimate future benefits. Here's how it works.

First, we need to make a list of our best features and benefits. These are the things that provide the solutions for our prospects' problems. Once we have these identified, we can then add the phrase "so that" after each one.

For example, if our benefit is that we offer a money-back guarantee, immediately add the "so that" phrase. Now it sounds like this. "We have a money-back guarantee so that you will feel confident and never worry about losing money with your purchase."

By adding **"so that"** after our benefits, we remind ourselves to always keep our prospects in mind. We should focus on how our product, service, or opportunity can help them and make their lives easier.

Some more examples?

- Our 10-day weight loss program works fast so that you can look great at your high school reunion.
- People use our online ordering so that they can avoid the hassle and expense of local shopping.
- Team members love our weekly trainings so that they can improve their skills to go full-time quicker.
- We explain by online video so that you can learn at your own pace and on your schedule.

The best part of "so that" is that it forces us to be clear and concise in our benefits. No more boring sales talk. This forces us to think about why this benefit matters to our prospects.

Prospects don't buy stuff, they buy solutions to their problems.

The two-word marketing secret. "So that." By using this simple phrase, our prospects can see the value in what we offer.

These simple words keep us focused on our prospects.

But ... but ... is this the only two-word phrase that can do this?

Of course not!

Let's add these two words to our marketing tool belt. Ready?

"Which means."

"Which means" is an alternate phrase that works the same.

Here are four more examples.

- Our business is part-time, which means it won't interfere with our present job.
- Our business is low-cost, which means it is easy to get started.
- Our training is digital, which means you can watch it from anywhere.
- You can get started today, which means you don't have to wait to improve your life.

The two-word marketing secret? We can use "so that" or "which means" to make sure our features and benefits translate into valuable solutions for our prospects.

The benefit of the benefit

Prospects don't like to think. Thinking is hard work. But, we can help.

When we announce benefits in our offers, our prospects must think through how this might change their future. Why should we make them do all the work when we know how our benefits can improve their lives?

Let's do some fun examples. Plus, let's go even a step further. We will make a benefit of the benefit of the benefit. Why? Just because we can!

Weight loss tablets

Benefit: Lose weight fast.

Benefit of the benefit: Lose weight fast so you will look great in pictures.

Benefit of the benefit of the benefit: Lose weight fast so that you will look great in pictures, which means you will be more popular on dating sites.

Mobile phone plan

Benefit: Save money on your monthly mobile phone plan.

Benefit of the benefit: Save money on your monthly mobile phone plan so that your savings will pay for a better phone.

Benefit of the benefit of the benefit: Save money on your monthly mobile phone plan so that your savings will pay for a better phone, which means you will impress your clients that you are successful as you use your top-of-the-line phone.

Mobile phone

Benefit: You can use it anywhere instead of being stuck at home with your stationery rotary dial phone from the 1960s.

Benefit of the benefit: You can use it anywhere instead of being stuck at home with your stationery rotary dial phone from the 1960s, so that now you can see prospects in person.

Benefit of the benefit of the benefit: You can use it anywhere instead of being stuck at home with your stationery rotary dial phone from the 1960s, so that now you can see prospects in person, which means you will earn more money in commissions by ditching your old phone.

Part-time business opportunity

Benefit: Make money on the side.

Benefit of the benefit: Make money on the side so that you can pay for private school and the vacations your family loves.

Benefit of the benefit of the benefit: Make money on the side so that you can pay for private school and the vacations your family loves, which means you will feel great about being the provider for your family.

Be your own boss

Benefit: Work when you want.

Benefit of the benefit: Work when you want so that you can be home for your children's school activities and sports.

Benefit of the benefit of the benefit: Work when you want so that you can be home for your children's school activities and sports, which means they will have great memories growing up.

Prospects want the future

Too often we get consumed with the features and benefits of what we offer. Our prospects don't care about what we offer. They only care about what our offer can do for them. We want to present the outcome, and not the boring details of how we will get there.

That is why we use "so that" and "which means" to help us focus on how our offers can make a difference in our prospect's life. We help prospects picture a brighter future ... a future where families put their dreams on a to-do list, not a bucket list.

TOOL #6:
URGENCY

To procrastinate is human.

Very human.

Our minds are designed for now, not for the future. The present is urgent, the future … well, that is for another time. The future is something for "future me" to worry about.

Since we make offers to humans, we want to increase their urgency for action. If we don't, then our prospects delay and miss out on the benefits of our offer.

We are not talking fake urgency here. We will not say, "This secret offer is only good for the next 17 minutes. If you miss out, you will miss it forever!"

Prospects can smell insincerity. And this 17-minute offer smelled.

Innocent questions that focus prospects to make decisions—now!!!

A better, more humane way of using urgency is to focus our prospects on this question, "How much longer do I want to continue living with this problem?

Remember listening?

The more painful the problem is for our prospects, the higher their motivation will be to take action. Assuming we heard a real problem from our prospects, a painful problem they want to solve, the main problem we will have to address is their procrastination.

The solution?

Questions.

An example?

We are sitting across from the prospects at their kitchen table. They are afraid to make a decision. They think:

- "We don't want to make a mistake."
- "I can't do anything until after the holidays."
- "What if we make the wrong decision?"
- "Let me wait until I have some free time."
- "Let's think it over and delay any decision until we have to."
- "What if we fail?"
- "Maybe we should take our time thinking about this."
- "When the kids grow up, then it will be a better time to think about this."

They continue to think in circles. If only they would make a decision, any decision, it would be wonderful. We could go home. They could get on with their lives.

But no, that would be too easy.

Our prospects insist on torturing themselves with indecision. They don't realize that "not making a decision" is making a decision to keep things "just as they are."

Yes, delaying is making a decision to keep their problem

For example, if a train is in the station and we don't know if we should board or not, if we think, think, think … the train leaves the station. Our indecision made a decision: we're not going to be on that train.

We know this, but our prospects don't. They don't realize this reality when they delay making decisions. Delaying is making a decision to keep their lives the same. Keeping their lives the same is okay, but they should consciously make that decision, not by default.

So, here are several innocent, non-aggressive questions that we can ask our prospects to help them make a conscious decision on what is best for their lives. Ready?

"What will happen if you don't join our business?"

Of course, the answer is "nothing." But we don't answer that question. We allow the prospects to mentally answer that question for themselves. They'll probably think this:

"Life will be the same. Tomorrow will look like today. We're going to wake up early, commute to work, come home late, grab a quick meal, watch a few minutes of television, kiss our sleeping kids good night, and go to sleep. Yep, we're going to live this soulless routine over and over again – until we're too old to work."

Not a very pretty picture, is it? If our prospects choose to leave everything the same, if they choose to avoid our opportunity, that's okay. They are making a decision, and that's all we ask.

Now for a few more questions like this. Let's see if one of these questions fits our style.

- "If you don't start your own business now, do you see yourself always working for someone else?"

- "Do we want to risk our financial future by having all of our income in one place?"

- "What will happen to our skin if we don't protect it from wrinkles?"

- "How will we get by with the increasing prices if we don't have a second income?"

- "What do you think will happen next year if you decide not to make any changes this year?"

- "What will happen if we don't go on a diet and begin to lose this weight?"

- "Do you think your job routine (five days a week, two weeks vacation every year) will ever change?"

- "I see that you're stressing about risking a change in your daily life. Why not just relax and enjoy your life as it is?"

- "You don't have to make a decision to start your own business tonight. Instead, you could make a decision not to start your own business and keep your present job routine."

- "You might be thinking, 'My daily routine isn't so bad. Maybe I'll keep living this way.' That's also a good decision. Do you think that might be best for you?"

- "So what is going to happen if you don't fix this problem?"

These questions remind our prospects that the pain of their problems won't go away by procrastinating their decision. Now they must make a conscious decision about their future.

And remember, this technique is rejection-free. We're not attached to the outcome. We're not responsible for the decisions they make for their lives. We're only obligated to give our prospects the choices. The rest is up to them.

Ultimately, we want to make clear that our offer is, "You can take advantage now of this wonderful offer, or do nothing. And nothing means keeping your problems."

Can we use scarcity to motivate our prospects to take action?

Sincere scarcity? Yes.

Fake scarcity? No.

Let's think of scarcity as a reason to take action now, not an artificial manipulation. We don't want to manipulate or deceive our prospects.

Scarcity can mean setting limits for what we offer. For example:

- We only have a limited amount of weeks to qualify for this upcoming incentive trip or this month's rank advancements. Let's start qualifying now. We don't want to lose any more days.

- If we want to quit our job in January, we only have five more months to get our business into action.

- This is our company's annual two-for-one offer. They do it for the month, so now is the time to take advantage of this special offer.

- The company does this special skin care training certification three times a year. If we don't join and register now, we will have to wait four more months before we have another chance.

- We only get a few years of retirement before we die. If we could retire early, we could get more years.

- We have to qualify at this rank within 90 days of joining to win this free trip.

- Inaction now could mean a lost opportunity.

- They discontinued this item, so these are the only ones remaining.

- There is a 50% off product launch special from the company that ends this evening.

Think of scarcity not as manipulation, but more as a call to action. The time to make a decision is now. No one wants to have default decisions defining their lives.

What if our prospects don't respond to our "call to action" or make a decision?

It might be a hint.

Maybe our offer isn't solving an urgent problem. Problems motivate prospects more than benefits. And future benefits will have even less impact on our prospects.

The best urgency is for "now" problems.

Future problems?

Prospects procrastinate and assign that problem to their future self. Nothing to worry about right now.

Offers that solve immediate problems have more power than offers that promise future benefits.

But, let's look at a possible conversation we could have with our stalling prospects. Maybe they need a bit of a nudge to finally take action and fix their problem.

Prospect: "Yes, I need more money, but I am so busy. No way I can do anything now. Plus, I would need more time to think this over."

Us: "You mentioned you had this problem for a long time, and I know you have been thinking of solutions to fix this problem. Would you agree that you will have to take care of this problem sometime in the future?"

Prospect: "Yes, I will have to earn more money. But like I said, I am busy now."

Us: "What does your future look like? Do you think you will be busy in the future?"

Prospect: "Probably. I use up all my 24 hours every day. Everyone depends on me."

Us: "Since you have so many obligations now, I am sure you will always be busy. Why not take a small step now to get started, as you will always be busy in the future?"

Prospect: "Hmmm. How small of a step could we take?"

And now we begin to design the solution.

How to continue the conversation.

When our prospects delay and refuse to make a decision, but we want to keep the conversation open for possibilities, we could say this:

"Okay. What do you think would be a good next step?"

Now it is our prospects' turn to talk and suggest an action.

Will it work every time? No. But we should give our prospects a chance to suggest an alternative option, and this prompts them to think of their future.

TOOL #7:
CALL TO ACTION

Newton's First Law: Inertia

"An object at rest remains at rest, and an object in motion remains in motion at constant speed and in a straight line unless acted on by an unbalanced force."

We only have to worry about the first part of this law. Our prospects are at rest. They need a push to go into action. We have to tell them exactly what action to take now.

What are some actions we can suggest?

Register now and get started

- Start by buying this package
- Get on a three-way call with our sponsor
- Press the order button now
- Let's do it
- Just go to:
- Get your free …
- Partner up now
- Don't leave me behind
- Put me on the list

We can't depend on our prospects' initiative to take the next step. We must describe the next step, and let them know now is the time to take that step.

This sounds great, but how do we do this? How do we suggest action without begging or pressure?

Remember, our prospects have the option of taking advantage of our wonderful offer … or deciding not to take our wonderful offer and continue with their current lives. Their choice.

Here are some suggested rejection-free wordings we can use.

- Does it make sense to start now, so we can start the countdown to firing your boss?

- You told me you have been thinking about this problem for six months already. Well, now that we know a solution, what do you want to do? Fix this problem now, or do nothing and keep the problem?

- Are you okay with continuing to keep this problem? Or is now a good time to finally fix this problem?

- Let's start now by trying this product. Then, in one month you will know if it will work for you or not.

- So this is how everything works. You can take action to get started now, or you can do nothing and keep your situation the same. You choose what is best.

- Well, this will fix your problem. We can order it today. Or, you can choose not to fix your problem. That is a choice also.

- I will tell you about our business, but when I do, please know that it is up to you. You can choose to keep your life the same. No problem. Or, you can choose to join our business, and work to earn that extra money you need.

- You don't have to do anything and things will remain the same, or if you are ready to change your situation, let's get started now.

- It is okay to make a decision now to keep your current situation, but it is also okay to start our business now.

One of my favorite openings?

If we don't want to appear pushy or have an agenda, then we can open our presentation with these words:

"I have two offers. The first offer is easy. Don't do anything, keep your current life and everything the same.

"The second offer is to take advantage of this part-time business and have that extra money you need.

"Now, I don't know which offer will be best for you. Only you know your circumstances. So, if you want, I can explain how offer #2 works."

We know what we offer is an improvement to our prospects' lives, but they will need a prompt of what to do to get started. That is why prospects need us.

Procrastination is the natural state of our prospects. We are there to help them take that first step.

How can I make this option close sound more natural?

Early, when introducing our offer, we could say this:

"It is okay to keep your problem, but it is also okay to use this option to fix your problem. Let me explain this option."

Now, our prospects are primed in advance to make a decision. They know they will have to make a choice, to take action … or not.

"Two choices sound good, but are there exceptions?"

Of course. Giving two choices represents "best practices" to get instant decisions. But, sometimes we see more than two choices. Why?

Here is a classic example of using three choices to funnel a decision to a preferred choice. Ready?

We spend the hot day walking in an outside open market shopping for entertainment. Now we are thirsty.

Ah, a soft drink stand ahead. Excellent.

The choices? Small, medium, and large.

- $3 for the small drink. Hmmm. That seems expensive but we are thirsty. This is the only place offering drinks. Seems okay.

- $5.50 for a medium drink. A bit more than we want to pay for, even if we are extremely thirsty.

- $5.99 for the large drink. More than we need, but compared to $5.50 for the medium drink, the large drink is a bargain.

And what size drink will we walk away with?

The large drink, of course. It was a bargain!

The medium drink was $2.50 more than the tiny, expensive small drink. And the large drink was only 49 cents more than the medium drink. The large drink is an absolute steal!

As professionals in making offers, this scene bothers us. So we spend time watching the steady stream of thirsty buyers, one after another, line up and pay … $5.99 for the large drinks.

This soft drink stand is making a fortune selling $5.99 soft drinks to eager buyers.

What is their secret?

Small minds have trouble with three options

First, forget logic. It is too hard for us to juggle three different choices in our small minds. Remember, it is hard for us to keep a single thought at work in our minds. No room for a second thought. Plus, we want to forget our present thoughts and move on to our next interesting thoughts. Yeah, our minds are a disorganized mess.

Well, if we can't juggle three options in our minds at the same time, then what do we do?

We default to comparing two options at a time. This is easier for us. And that is why we think, "Hey! For only 49 cents more I can have this gigantic, enormous large drink instead of that medium drink. What a bargain!"

Then, we justify our decision. We tell ourselves, "Wow. Look at this bargain. Look at all the money we are saving. We'll need this extra drink as we are not done shopping yet. Now we won't have to stop again to look for drinks."

What mind bias causes this phenomenon?

Our minds fear paying more. But, our minds fear making a mistake more than our minds fear paying more. And the mistake? Oh, that would be buying a drink that is too small and doesn't quench our thirst. Yes, that would be a loss of our $3. We don't want to lose.

So our bias tells us, "It is okay to pay a little more to make sure we don't lose."

The secret is in the less attractive option

In the soft drink example, the middle choice, the $5.50 medium-sized drink, is not a good option. Why?

First, the medium drink is a lot more expensive when compared to the small drink.

Second, the medium drink is almost as expensive as the large drink, but the large drink is so much larger, so much better value.

Adding the middle, less attractive option forces our minds to compare the small drink with the large drink. Now it gets messy. Our brain starts to unwind. We talk to ourselves:

"We don't want to pay $2.50 more for an inferior-sized drink when we can get a much larger one for only 49 cents more. And what if we get thirsty later? And how much better is the large drink in value per ounce? Uh, math. Our head hurts. But it looks like a better deal."

We order a large-sized drink. Seems safer.

Adding an inferior option affects decisions. In marketing, this is called the "Decoy Effect."

Barhopping strategy

This is why single people go barhopping with a slightly less attractive friend. It is easier for them to be compared with their slightly less attractive friend next to them. Quicker decisions. Better chance for a date.

The lesson is clear. Prospects like to compare two choices. But introducing a third choice makes things fuzzy, unless we make the extra choice less attractive. Then, this unattractive third choice will influence the final choice.

So let's do a couple of examples for our network marketing businesses.

Example #1: Start-up packs.

A. $59 start-up pack.
B. $99 start-up pack with free products.
C. $99 start-up pack with free products and free back office for a year.

Which choice is unattractive? Choice B. Yeah, Choice B is stupid.

Which choice will be chosen most often by our prospects? Choice C.

Example #2: Start-up packs.

A. Pay the retail price for our products.
B. Become a preferred customer for $89 one-time and buy our products at wholesale forever.
C. Become a distributor for $99. Get our products at wholesale prices and earn bonuses and commissions when sharing with others.

Which choice is more attractive? Choice C.

Which choice is unattractive? Choice B.

And the result? More prospects will choose Choice C because we introduce an unattractive Choice B in our offer. It was easy for our prospects to compare the B and C choice.

Weird? Maybe. But it is how our flawed human brains think.

Adding an extra unattractive option will influence our prospects' decisions toward our preferred option.

Restaurant menu pricing now makes more sense

The smaller price difference between the appetizer size and the entree size now makes sense. They want us to upgrade to the entree size.

Fast food? Think combo meals. Want fries with that? The combo comes with a small drink.

The lesson?

Want our prospects to take action?

Then two choices are best. It is easier for humans to compare two things.

If we do introduce a third choice, make sure one of the choices is unattractive. The unattractive choice will influence the final choice.

But more about only two choices

Curious why two choices are best and how to do it?

Then, let's continue.

TOOL #8:
"A CONFUSED MIND
ALWAYS SAYS ... NO!"

Simplicity. Fewer choices. Less head trash and complicated offers.

The Cheesecake Factory's menu is over 20 pages long with over 250 items to choose from. That is mind-numbing.

Sure, variety is a sales benefit, but think of the stress of balancing the different choices for our meals.

Compare this to the local hot dog truck. The only choice is French Fries or not.

Ask ourselves, which decision is easier? The Cheesecake Factory's menu or the hot dog truck? The answer is obvious.

Human minds like easy decisions. Holding too many options inside of our heads only confuses us.

So how many choices should we give our prospects?

The ideal number of choices is ... two.

As we saw, adding a third option, the choice becomes more complicated for our prospects.

Too many choices will induce analysis paralysis. Our prospects think, "Do I want to hurt my brain thinking through all these complicated options, or do I want to put off the decision to the future."

And we know what happens next. Prospects put off their decision.

Here are some quick examples of only two choices:

1. Renting vs. buying a home
2. Taking public transportation vs. driving your own car
3. Investing in stocks or putting money into a savings account
4. Going out for dinner or cooking at home
5. Paper or plastic bags at the grocery store

… and taking advantage of our wonderful offer … or our prospects continuing their miserable lives without the benefits of our wonderful offer.

In these examples, the choices are clear and limited. With fewer choices, prospects can make decisions faster and easier.

So, instead of offering three different packages to join, we make it easy for our prospects. We give them the choice of buying this package, or missing out on our opportunity.

How would this sound in real life?

To our prospects, we could say, "So, what is it going to be easier for you? To get started with our program tonight so next year you can fire the boss? Or to continue working at this job you hate until you retire?"

Two choices.

There is no thinking it over. We didn't give them a "think it over and delay" choice.

So, when possible, let's give our prospects only two options when we make our offers. It is easier for them to make their choice.

Here is the easy fill-in-the-blank formula for two choices.

"So what is going to be easier for you?" (Tells them they must choose.)

Then, the choices.

- "Our wonderful offer?"
- "Or to keep your problems and continue life the same?"

And it doesn't even matter which choice comes first.

Here are some quick examples.

"So what is going to be easier for you? To continue exercising, eating funny foods and starving yourself, and watching the weight keep coming back? Or, to have our diet breakfast shake every morning, and watch the weight melt away?"

- "So what is it going to be easier for you? To continue over-paying for your electricity bill, or they take four minutes now and fix that problem forever."

- "So what is going to be easier for you? To start a part-time business now, so you will have an extra check next week? Or, to continue trying to get by on one paycheck?"

- "So what is going to be easier for you? To take care of your skin and feed it from the inside, so it continues to look young? Or, to continue wrinkling a little bit more every evening." (Okay, maybe a bit too far.)

- "So what's going to be easier for you? To over-caffeinate for your energy? Or, to use our nutritious energy drink where these healthy nutrients act like tiny cheerleaders giving you a standing ovation for hours."

- "So what is going to be easier for you? To keep battling with your unruly hair, looking like a poodle caught in a tornado? Or to use our taming hair conditioner and look like a supermodel every time you wash your hair?"

- "So what is going to be easier for you? To keep waking up feeling like a zombie from a B-grade horror movie? Or, to use our 'Good Night' herbal capsules for a great sleep every night?"

- "So what is it going to be easier for you? To continue being a human buffet for those blood-sucking mosquitos? Or, to repel those hungry insects with our essential oil anti-mosquito blend?"

- "So what is it going to be easier for you? To keep living in a world without rainbows, unicorns, and joy? Or, to drink our 'Happy Coffee' and make every day a great day?"

Two choices.

1. Our wonderful offer.
2. Do nothing and keep life's struggles.

Prospects love simplicity. When things get too complicated with too many moving parts to consider, we avoid taking action. We are not sure what we should do.

Let's make our offers easy and fast for our prospects to decide.

TOOL #9:
PRIMING

Priming in sales helps us influence the mindset of our prospects. It is a way to get prospects to look at our offers from a new point of view.

Think about our prospects. They have a problem, but they haven't solved it yet. They need a different way to look at their problem.

We can tell a short story or examples that give our prospects a new outlook on their problems and solutions.

The secret?

To tell this priming phrase or story before we present our offer. This is the time of least resistance from our prospects.

Try this. Before a presentation, ask, "Are you more of a 'reasons why' or more of a 'reasons why not' person?"

Most people want to impress us with their positivity and vision. They answer, "I am a 'reasons why' person."

They will want to prove this to us by being more positive when seeing our presentation.

Here is an example of what we could tell a minimum wage worker with a minimum wage mindset. His $20-an-hour salary has given him a certain point-of-view about money.

But, why would we tell this story first?

Because if we didn't, our minimum wage worker, with his minimum wage mindset, would instantly reject our offer to join our network marketing business. He would say, "$100 to start a part-time business? Are you crazy? I need more money, I don't want to spend more money! That is crazy!"

The story

We sit down with this minimum wage prospect earning $20 an hour, and ask this question:

"If your grandmother died and left you $1,000, how would you invest it?"

Now we listen to his possible answers:

#1. I would definitely buy some new video games with that kind of windfall. It's not every day you come into some extra cash, you know?

#2. I read that I should invest in stocks. A good return would be 10%, but hey, I am talented. I will get a 20% annual return. I will turn that $1,000 investment into $1,200. Hedge fund managers would be jealous.

#3. I would invest the $1,000 into cryptocurrency and trading forex. I heard that was the way to instant wealth. I would probably double or triple my money. Let all those professional traders be the losers. Now I would have $2,000 or $3,000 in one year. I am an investment guru!

Our minimum wage prospect reveals his awareness of business and investing. Now, we know where to start our explanation so we can relate to our prospect.

So what is the best answer to this question?

The best answer is to invest the $1,000 in yourself. That is the biggest payoff. And, that payoff is for the rest of our lives.

For example, if our prospect invested the $1,000 into some bookkeeping courses at the local community college, he could double his salary from $20 an hour to a $40 an hour bookkeeper rate. That is $40,000 more in one year!

After explaining this solution to our minimum wage prospect, then we listen.

If our prospect "gets it" that investing in ourselves is a better choice, now learning new skills and starting a new network marketing business makes sense.

At this point, we can introduce our network marketing business to our prospect and his new mindset about investing in himself.

Does priming instantly change viewpoints?

Yes. Here is an easy example.

The tour guide tells us a little story about snakes. If we are like most humans, we have a healthy fear of snakes, especially venomous snakes.

What will we be thinking about as we take a walk through the jungle?

Snakes!

Will our pulse rate go up as we move through waist-high grass where we can't see our feet?

Our entire thinking is about snakes.

Priming works.

Can I make priming even easier?

Absolutely!

In a sentence or two, we can completely change how our prospects will view our offer. Here is an example of what we could say to a jobholder.

- "There is an old saying that having a job guarantees we will be broke. Having our own business is the only true way to get ahead."

Now our prospect is primed to see starting a business as a real opportunity instead of an expense.

To see a new path in life, prospects need to look with a different point of view. We can adjust their vision with priming. For example, if we think our prospect might be a procrastinator, we could say this before we start:

- "There is never a convenient time to build your dreams."

Or maybe this for people who claim to be too busy to get ahead:

- "There are only 24 hours in a day. We have to give up something to gain something."

These statements will lessen the chances of a procrastination excuse at the end of our presentation.

Need a few more examples of priming?

- "If we don't take care of our body, then where are we going to live?"
- "Our face is our best first impression. And we only get one chance!"

- "The best time to start a business was 20 years ago. The second best time is now!"

- "The more action we take, the luckier we get in life."

- "When we invest in ourselves, it is not an expense. It's an investment that yields returns for a lifetime."

- "Of course, if we don't take the first step towards our dreams, they will never become reality."

- "We want natural and safe products for our homes because we live there."

- "It's not about having a plan for today or tomorrow; it's about having a plan for life!"

- "Smart people take care of their skin from the inside as well as from the outside."

- "We can use superfoods that are so nutritious, our veggies will get jealous."

- "Smart people can do math. They know that paying less makes good sense."

- "Why wait for an opportunity when we can create it ourselves?"

- "No matter how small our first step is, as long as we keep moving forward we will reach our destination."

- "We have to give up something to gain something."

This gets to be too much fun!

Our offer will get better acceptance when we prime our prospects with a point of view.

Humans have a program that goes like this:

"I am right. What I believe is true. And once I tell you my viewpoint, I don't want to embarrass myself by changing my viewpoint. I don't want to appear weak-willed, stupid, or flakey."

Which means … once our prospects agree with our priming statement, they will insist on keeping this belief during our conversation. Less stress for us. Now we don't have to sell and convince prospects as they think the same way we do.

Want more power?

Let's use the magic words phrase, "There is an old saying …"

By placing this phrase before any fact, the fact must be true. Now our priming statement feels easier to accept by our prospects. Some examples using the above statements?

- "There is an old saying that if we don't take care of our body, then where are we going to live?"
- "There is an old saying that our face is our best first impression. And we only get one chance!"
- "There is an old saying that the best time to start a business was 20 years ago. The second best time is now!"
- "There is an old saying that the more action we take, the luckier we get in life."

The magic is before our offer. With open-minded prospects, everything gets easier. (That's an old saying.)

Let's prime a prospect by telling the following story

We can tell a short story before we present our opportunity. There is little or no rejection or stress before our presentation. Why? Because our prospects want to hear how our story ends.

Here is an example.

You know, I get to talk to many people about my business. I notice that the people I talk to fall into one of these four groups.

#1. he people who want to get rich without doing anything. No work, no investment. They want to sit on their butts and hope they get rich.

#2. The people who talk and talk, but never take action. They always have a new plan or get-rich ideas, but never take the first step. They find it easier to just talk.

#3. The people who want to start a part-time business while still keeping their day job. They want the safety net of an extra income, without risking giving up the security of their current job.

#4. The crazy people. They take giant risks, quit their jobs, jump in without looking, and dream about a successful business.

Anyway, I hope you and I can agree that group #3, the people who start part-time to give their family a financial safety net, have the best chance to get ahead.

But first, let me show you how this part-time business works.

• • •

Now our prospects are primed for a realistic look at a part-time business to improve their lives.

Priming with fear of loss

Here are more short stories.

• • •

Us: "Let's do a math test. Imagine we earn $6,000 a month from our job, but we want to be earning $10,000 a month. What is that gap in income costing us every month? Let's do some quick math."

"It costs us $4,000 a month."

"Yes, we are losing $4,000 every month that we delay fixing this problem."

• • •

Us: "Do you think inflation is going to go up or down?"

Prospects: "Always up."

Us: "So next year we will need to get an extra job, just to avoid falling further behind. That doesn't sound like fun, does it?"

• • •

There is always a risk when we move forward, but there is also a risk when we stay where we are.

For example, what if we never wanted to change and kept our rotary phones from the 1960s? Our decision not to risk change would prevent us from keeping in touch with our grandchildren, and of course, we would feel embarrassed that we didn't join the 21st century.

• • •

Priming is fun. We want our prospects to have an open mind before we present.

TOOL #10:
ANCHORING

Anchoring is a cognitive bias where we rely heavily on the first piece of information. We use this as a reference point to compare things.

This is an effective way of managing our prospects' expectations. Our prospects' mindset is important when they hear our price. Remember, our price is not only the amount of money spent, but also the effort, and the risk involved.

Want to see anchoring in action?

Go shopping for clothes. Only amateur shoppers pay retail prices.

Most retail stores do this. They mark down the retail price to show a sale price.

What does this sale price signal to our brains?

"Oh, this item is on sale from a much higher price. It must be a bargain to get such an expensive item at this low price."

We mentally assign a higher value to this item. The store successfully "anchored" the value of this item at a higher price in our mind, thereby making the sale price attractive.

What about us?

We want to meet or exceed our prospects' expectations. Let's use a money example first.

Imagine our prospects expect that our offer will cost $25. If they discover our offer will cost $50, our prospects will be disappointed.   But what if our prospects expect our offer to cost $50, but then discover our offer is only $25? Then, we meet or exceed our prospects' expectations. Our prospects feel better.

Anchoring works because we can influence the expectations of our prospects. How?

With a story.

Before introducing the price or cost of what we offer, let's tell a short story about the benefits of our offer first. This story can set the expectations of the value of our offer.

Here is an example of the cost of starting our network marketing business.

"My friend, Joe, decided to go into business. He took a huge mortgage on his home and bought an expensive franchise for $500,000. A big risk. But most of us don't want to take that kind of risk with our family's money. Instead, we prefer to start our business part-time, while still keeping our jobs. Our network marketing business can do that. And the good news is that it only costs $500 to start."

The story helps to anchor our prospects' mindsets. We create the expectation that the price to start a business is huge. Our offer of $500 feels like a deal because it meets or exceeds their expectations.

An example of a children's nutrition product?

"We know these nutrients are essential for our child's growth. But if we were to buy these ingredients separately, we would spend over $300 a month at the health food store. Ouch. That is why we combined these ingredients in tasty gummies for kids that cost only $49 a month. Now children can get all the nutrition they need."

By anchoring the cost of buying the individual ingredients, we manage our prospects' expectations. When they find out that it is only $49 a month, they feel like they got a great deal.

Anchoring helps us to create effective offers and influence our prospects' expectations … before making their decisions. We can test different stories and prices to determine what works best for our offer.

Rolls-Royce and the anchoring bias at work

Rory Sutherland tells the story of Rolls-Royce marketing their cars. A £300,000+ car is not exactly an easy thing to sell. There are plenty of other things prospects could do with £300,000.

So what did Rolls-Royce do?

They displayed their cars at yacht and aircraft shows.

"If you've been looking at jets all morning, a £300,000 car is an impulse buy. It's like putting sweets next to the counter" — Rory Sutherland

Oh. And yet network marketers complain that their bottles of vitamins are too expensive. Maybe a bit of positioning and anchoring could help.

So how can I anchor my products?

How can I anchor my business startup costs?

Start by talking about something more expensive first

This is how our human minds work. We understand new things by comparing them to something we already know. We want to look like a less expensive, more attractive option.

What if we are not less expensive? We could show that we are more convenient.

The good news is that we get to pick what we decide to compare with.

Here are ten examples

#1. Business opportunity

Talk about the costs of renting office space or hiring expensive consultants. We could talk about our fear of the unknown licenses and permits we must get. Even a franchise could cost hundreds of thousands.

Then, show that it only costs $599 to start our business, and we don't have to rent expensive office space or quit our jobs.

#2. Jewelry

Show pictures and the prices of expensive jewelry. Talk about the investment costs and the insurance needed.

Then, display the wide variety of fashion jewelry one could have for less than the cost of a single expensive ring.

#3. Skincare

Start the conversation with the costs and pain for plastic surgery and Botox.

Now our skincare products look like a bargain.

#4. Nutritional products

What is the cost of being sick? Do we miss paychecks? Do we pay for expensive doctor visits? Get our prospects to start putting price tags on these costs.

Then, our nutritional products won't seem as expensive.

#5. Hair care

A single professional salon treatment for damaged hair can cost upwards of $300 per session.

We can now prevent damaged hair and have salon-quality results for much less.

#6. Water purification

Ask if our prospects drink bottled water. If they do, then show them a picture of two years' worth of empty plastic water bottles. Maybe mention that bottled water may not even be purified.

Having a water purification system at home saves us from carrying water bottles, and we then know the quality of the water we are drinking.

#7. Essential oils

Cost of camping? Travel costs, campsite costs, hours of travel, and sleeping on the ground. Ugh.

Essential oils? Fill the home with the fresh, natural scent of the outdoors for only a tiny percentage of the cost, plus the comfort of our own beds. Full air conditioning and heat on demand.

#8. Weight-loss products

Gym memberships. Expensive personal trainers. Dangerous liposuction surgeries.

Or, a few tablets and protein drinks for less. No pain either.

#9. Energy drinks

Ask our prospects if they buy fancy coffees. If they do, add up the costs over a month or two. Talk about travel time or waiting in line.

Now our energy-on-demand energy drinks seem more affordable and convenient.

#10. Identity theft

How much will it cost in time and energy to reverse those fraudulent credit card charges? And how are we going to prove to the bank over the phone that we really are not a scammer? If our credit rating gets destroyed, future financing and jobs might be impossible.

But one simple phone call to fix everything? That sounds like a bargain!

Expensive? Difficult? Compared to what?

Anchor a higher cost in our prospects' minds first. This will be the most recent memory in our prospects' minds. And remember, we get to choose what we will ultimately compare our offers with.

Then, with the higher costs anchored in our prospects' minds, our offers will shine as an alternate option.

TOOL #11: HUMANS ARE SHORT-TERM THINKERS

Now … is more powerful than later. It is easier for us to think of our next step than to plan far ahead into the future.

Not a long-term thinker?

Relax. That's normal. For tens of thousands of years, humans died young. We didn't have much need to plan for the future. Cavemen didn't have to worry about their 401K retirement plan.

So the natural tendency is for us to want immediate rewards.

Let's do a test. What choices do you think people will make?

A. An immediate bonus check, or
B. A residual income in the future?

A. To go on a 90-day contest, or
B. Try a one-day contest?

A. An instant income tax refund, or
B. Wait months for the government to process the tax return.

A. To eat this tasty pizza now, or
B. Worry about our long-term cholesterol test at next year's annual physical?

A. Put money in a long-term retirement savings account, or
B. Go on a shopping spree?

A. Put a bit more into an emergency fund for unexpected events, or
B. Buy something exciting right now?

A. Get the latest smartphone now, or
B. Wait years to save up for it?

A. Purchase an expensive car to impress our friends, or
B. Drive our rusty car and invest in a secure retirement plan?

A. Spend social time watching television with family and friends, or
B. Work overtime to earn more money?

A. Cook a complicated home meal after a long day at work, or
B. Throw something in the microwave?

Do we see a pattern yet?

We make our offers more attractive if we focus on now. Long-term benefits are nice, but not as powerful in our prospects' minds.

So how can we take advantage of this?

We can lead with immediate gratification, and then add on a few sentences about long-term benefits.

For example, we can emphasize the fast-start bonuses in our business opportunity, but also mention that they are building a residual income at the same time.

Or, we can emphasize the first week's expected weight loss, and then mention a longer-term outcome.

Or, we can emphasize how good our skin will feel tomorrow with this overnight skincare, and then mention the anti-aging effect.

We don't have to forget our long-term benefits, but prospects enjoy it more when they can see short-term results first.

But ... but ... it takes time to build our business, so what can I tell my prospects?

What would be an immediate short-term benefit they could experience?

How about the feeling of hope tomorrow morning as they commute to their job? Instead of that desperate feeling from that job they hate, they could feel great that they are on their way to financial freedom.

If our prospects want sooner instead of later, let's do our best to emphasize the short-term benefits of our offer.

TOOL #12: PROBLEMS ROCK!

Ask ourselves, "When we talk to our prospects, what should we talk about?"

Think about our lives. Do we want a residual income? Do we want to be our own boss? Are we excited about the benefits of our business? Enjoy winning incentive trips?

Yes!

However, this morning our car does not start.

What is on our minds?

The future of our business, or that our car will not start?

Problems take priority in our minds

At this moment we don't think about qualifying for our next bonus. We don't think about the upcoming trip for leaders.

Instead, the problem of our car not starting dominates our minds.

It is the same with our prospects.

Problems dominate their minds.

If we want to be #1 in our prospects' minds, we must talk about their problems. Benefits? That is something for later.

Life's daily stream of emergencies and predicaments show up 10X as much as do future benefits on our prospects' radar screens.

Problems control our prospects' attention. Everything else fades into the background.

That is why when we talk about our company's features and benefits, our prospects might not be listening. They are pondering their many problems.

What is the most important and most interesting subject to our prospects? They are. And when we talk about them and their problems, they hang on our every word. Our message gets spotlighted in the front of their minds.

Prove it!

Imagine we offer a wonderful winter coat. It is a beautiful winter coat. Many pockets and it's very fashionable. The color? It is the latest trend.

Now today is a cold winter day. We ask people passing by on the street, "Would you like to buy this beautiful winter coat? It is better than your coat right now. So many extra benefits."

Will some people buy it? Possibly. But most will rush by us. Offering more benefits is hard to do.

What is easier?

Solving a problem.

So, on this cold winter day, we ask shivering people passing by on the street who don't have a coat, "Would you like to buy this beautiful winter coat?"

Can we expect to make more sales? Of course!

People with problems have more motivation to listen and take action.

So, whenever possible, let's try to solve problems.

And what if they don't think their problems are big enough?

We can help.

It's easy to get prospects to focus on their problems more. Just a few questions is all it takes. For example:

- How long have you had this problem?
- Do other people know how much you suffer with this problem?
- What is the biggest inconvenience with this problem?
- If you could solve this problem, what would happen?

If you're the type of person that engages in a lot of drama, you will be very good at this enhancing their pain awareness. It is easy to get people to talk about how much they suffer. They love it.

Problems first

When we make offers to our prospects, let's try to focus on their problems. That is where their attention is.

When our prospects have a problem, it is easy to talk to them. We won't need superstar persuasive skills. We won't have to high-pressure them to pay attention to us.

Instead, we will find an eager and receptive audience for our offers.

Save the benefits, company history, and compensation plan details for later. We want an instant "yes" decision for our offers.

TOOL #13: MORE VALUE IS BETTER THAN DISCOUNTS

Our upline sales leader screams, "Don't discount! Charge full retail prices!"

Okay. Sounds good, but we ask, "How do we do it? My prospects think our products are too expensive. They feel I'm trying to make money off of them. Even our wholesale prices are high. They ask for big discounts or they won't even get a trial order. So what should I say?"

The upline sales leader pauses, then pauses some more. "Well, uh, well, just don't give discounts."

That wasn't helpful.

It is easy to give advice, but harder to give solutions.

Every potential customer wants a deal. No surprise here.

But, instead of fighting prospects over prices, let's take a look at what is happening inside our prospects' minds.

Ready?

Here is a secret.

Prospects buy because they feel that buying what we offer is better than not buying

It is not about price, features, power games, discounting, artificial scarcity, or the secret over-priced bonuses if they buy now before our imaginary deadline. It isn't the 1980s anymore.

Our prospects buy if the value we offer will exceed the price they will pay. Our selfish prospects do things for their own self-interests.

So that is the secret. Make sure our prospects see and feel the big value we offer.

It's not the price

If discounts were the reason prospects bought, then prospects would instantly change their utilities to the lowest-cost provider. Everyone would drive the cheapest automobile. No one would buy stylish shoes. Expensive handbag stores would be out of business. And, no one would order pizza for delivery.

Prospects buy for many reasons such as variety, uniqueness, image, utility, their relationship with the salesman, and even brand loyalty. A tiny discount won't make the difference. It is not whether it is $79 or $83 for a bottle of vitamins. Lowering our start-up cost from $499 to only $389 won't make a difference either. Nobody wants discounts on things they don't want.

Value rocks.

Why do we discount?

If we don't feel our products provide enough value for the money we ask, our first reaction is to offer a discount. This sends a bad signal to our prospects. If we don't believe in our product's value, why should they?

Sometimes we want to offer a discount to please our prospects. Everyone loves a discount. We want to be nice. But, the downside is that we cheapen our product's perception and create doubt in our prospects by discounting.

Instead, we want to educate our prospects on the tremendous value of what we offer. Then, our regular price will feel like a discount to them.

Let's create bigger value.

Sylvia sells her vitamins for $90 a bottle, a one-month supply. A challenge? Yes.

Her prospects complain they can buy a bottle of vitamins from the local health food store much cheaper. Should Sylvia give away her profit and discount her products? No.

Working for free means she will be out of business. Not a good choice.

What is Sylvia's other choice? Provide more value. Here is our conversation with Sylvia.

Big Al: "Do you have current, happy customers now?"

Sylvia: "Yes. Once they try my vitamins for a month, they feel a difference. But many won't try my vitamins. Some buy my vitamins, and don't take them regularly. Then they feel disappointed and won't reorder. Those people won't even answer the phone when I call them."

Big Al: "What do you do now to make sure people take their vitamins after they buy?"

Sylvia: "I call them once a week to coach and encourage them. If I can get them to buy, I follow up with these calls."

Big Al: "Free coaching and encouraging. That sounds great. Why not add that to your offer when selling to prospects? Prospects know that personal coaching is expensive."

Sylvia: "Okay. I am already doing it. Sure, I can add that to my offer."

Big Al: "Then, what will your new offer sound like when they ask for a discount?"

Sylvia: "Of course, you can get an ordinary bottle of generic low-quality vitamins at the local health food store. But, when you don't see results, you lose your money. Not with us. We don't short-change or cheat on ingredients. We invest in effective nutrients that work. And if you don't feel the difference, you are the final judge. You get all of your money back. Plus, this includes four personal mini-coaching calls to make sure you feel the difference. I know your health is important to you."

Now, what will her prospects think? Better quality ingredients, a money-back guarantee, and it includes four personal mini-coaching calls. And at only $90, this sounds better than gambling on a low-quality, generic bottle from the local store.

Let's stop cutting our profit and cheapening our offers with discounts. Let's add more value and show our belief in what we offer. We want to create irresistible offers for our prospects.

What if they didn't want to buy vitamins?

Then, we can point out the obvious. We compare what we offer with an alternative. Prospects have choices. Let's show them what their other choice might look like.

"Everyone wants to be healthy. Dying early is inconvenient. So what else can we do for our health?

"We can pay and join the local gym, hire a personal trainer, and exercise daily. Then, switch our diet to organic, plant-based foods. This will be a different shopping experience than our local supermarket. We can learn to cook these new foods in a way that will preserve their nutrition. And with practice, we can make them taste good.

"Unfortunately, many of us have jobs, families, and feel pressed for time. We can't do these disciplines daily. Yes, taking our vitamins is a shortcut. But we all want to be healthier."

Now, how many people do we know that will join the local gym, hire a personal trainer, exercise daily, switch to an organic, plant-based foods diet, will take the time to shop for these specialty foods, learn to cook these new foods, and learn to make them tasty … and do this daily?

How many? Hmmm. Maybe … zero? One weird person?

Not many for sure.

What are our prospects thinking now?

"Wow! That sounds expensive. I can't afford that much time at the gym. Who would watch my kids? And I ate at a health food restaurant once. Ugh! Double ugh! I needed a double cheeseburger to wipe the taste from my mouth. But taking vitamins … that's doable. Especially if it includes personal coaching to stay on track. Of course, I want to get healthier. Swallowing a couple of tablets fits my current lifestyle."

They know they don't have the time or the discipline for what we described. Yet, they still want to be healthier. So, taking vitamins with added coaching support sounds pretty appealing now, right?

By presenting the alternative, we show our prospects the value our vitamins offer.

But what about my business opportunity?

Can we create bigger value for our business? Of course. Let's do an example.

Joe presents his network marketing opportunity to a typical prospect. Only $499 to join, and that includes $499 in products, so wow! Seems like a great deal, but Joe's prospect resists. He complains, "I need to earn money, not spend money. That is a lot of money. I don't have an extra $499 right now. And, this seems awfully expensive for starting a business. Can you discount this? Or, since I will be earning extra money for you, could you pay part of it?"

Joe thinks, "Hmmm. My prospect doesn't realize the total value here. I need to do a better job of explaining all the value I am offering."

Joe replies,

"Sure! I understand you need to earn money instead of spending money. Let me explain everything that you get with the $499 package.

"First of all, this isn't just a business opportunity. You also receive expert network marketing training and coaching. Yes, that is included in your startup package. No need to hire an expensive personal coach to start.

"The company's back office takes care of delivering to your customers, your accounting, and you don't have to rent an office.

"Plus, you get $499 in products that you can sell, or use personally if you choose.

"Plus, you become eligible for team bonuses and incentives. You are now in business!"

Joe's prospect replies, "Okay. I see the total value now. Makes sense. This is a great chance for me to get into business."

Prospects want value for their money.

"I got this great idea to discount to ... free"

With a sudden stroke of genius, Ed creates his most amazing sales offer ever. He decides to gift a free trial of his product with only a small fee for shipping and handling.

Ed was so confident in his offer that he even added a catchy slogan, "Get my amazing product for free, just pay for a little shipping and handling, and the secret will be ours!"

The response?

Underwhelming. Crickets. Total silence.

What happened?

First problem? Skepticism. Ed's prospects thought the offer of the free gift sounded too good to be true.

Second problem? Ed's entire sales offer was a discount. It doesn't matter how much we discount if our prospects don't want or value what we offer. Ed forgot to promote the benefits of his amazing product.

Third problem? Ed's prospects reacted by saying, "Well, it's not much of a gift if we have to pay for shipping and handling, is it?"

Sometimes shortcuts can work, but this shortcut didn't.

More value will not help a boring offer that prospects don't want.

Think value first.

TOOL #14:
ADDING VALUE AND THE
CRINGY INFOMERCIAL

Insomnia? Let late-night infomercial offers put us to sleep.

Bored? Watch late-afternoon shopping channels with incredible offers on stuff we didn't know we needed.

Yeah, but do these infomercials work?

Yes. They don't do them for charity.

Do we have to be as obnoxious as these infomercials? No. But we can at least look at the tactics they use. But first, let's watch this imaginary infomercial for the Miracle Kitchen Gadget.

Grab our popcorn!

[Scene opens with a kitchen counter cluttered with random kitchen appliances and tools.]

Announcer: Tired of having to juggle multiple kitchen appliances to make a simple meal? Sick of spending hundreds of dollars on all those bulky, space-consuming gadgets piling up on your countertop? Well, fear not! Take a deep breath! Introducing the revolutionary new Miracle Kitchen Gadget that replaces every single item on your kitchen counter!

[Cut to a struggling mom preparing a meal with multiple kitchen gadgets.]

Fake Testimonial #1 (Southern country accent): "Before we got this miracle machine, we had to hire a babysitter to handle all our kitchen appliances. But now, we're saving money and time!"

Announcer: "That's right! This one gadget does it all! It slices, it dices, it chops, it grates, and it even sings a lullaby to your baby while you cook! And guess what? It's so easy and fun to use!"

[Cut to a happy mom using the Miracle Kitchen Gadget to prepare a meal while dancing to music.]

Fake Testimonial #2 (with a cheesy grin): "This Miracle Kitchen Gadget has changed my life! I used to have no time to dance around while cooking, but now I can do both at the same time! And the savings? Amazing!"

Announcer: "You heard it here, folks! And if you act now, you can get this miracle life-changing, marriage-saving device for only $100! That's a $700 savings compared to buying all those other kitchen gadgets!"

[Cut to a close-up of the Miracle Kitchen Gadget with a flashy graphic displaying the savings.]

Announcer: "But wait, there's more! Order in the next 24 hours, and we'll give you two of these special kitchen gadgets for the price of one! Yes! A second Miracle Kitchen Gadget for free! Unbelievable. We are breaking the laws of math just for you!"

[Cut to an excited family receiving a box with two Miracle Kitchen Gadgets.]

Fake Testimonial #3 (in a British accent): "I never thought I'd need more than one of these divine Miracle Kitchen Gadgets, but now I can cook for an entire royal wedding party with ease!"

Announcer: "And that's not all! Buy in the next hour, and we'll include our special collection of collectible royal look-alike spoons! These rare spoons have sold for over $300 elsewhere, but we'll include them with your order if you call in the next 60 minutes!"

[Cut to a close-up of the fancy royal look-alike spoons with a flashy graphic displaying their value.]

Announcer: "So, to summarize, you can replace every single item on your kitchen counter, save $700, get two Miracle Kitchen Gadgets, and collect some rare spoons all for only $100!"

[Cut to the device with a flashing "Call Now!" graphic.]

Announcer: "Don't miss out on this amazing opportunity! Call now and get cooking with ease and style! And remember, if you don't act fast, you'll be stuck with that cluttered kitchen counter forever! Don't be the only loser in your neighborhood that doesn't own a Miracle Kitchen Gadget and a set of royal look-alike spoons. So, call now!"

Do cringy infomercials work?

Yes.

We might grind our teeth when we watch these infomercials, but there is a market of buyers who enjoy the entertainment. They know the pitch. They know there will be a huge discount. They know they will get an extra one free. And they can't wait to see the extra bonus they add at the end.

These buyers would feel disappointed for anything less.

They don't want a boring PowerPoint presentation. They want cheesy, over-the-top, hype entertainment.

But the real question is:

Do our targeted prospects want a cheesy infomercial?

Probably not.

Our serious prospects might feel turned off by the hype. They might question the real value of our offer if we discount it so easily. They want value and substance, not cheesy entertainment.

What can we learn from this infomercial offer?

First, this infomercial does a great job of comparison. It establishes a problem and compares the present situation (crowded countertop of appliances) to their better solution (Miracle Kitchen Gadget). Remember, comparison is a great way to establish understanding and value.

Second, this infomercial uses strong, persuasive language.

Third, this informercial has a strong call to action. A little forced perhaps, but a call to act now. If someone hesitates, there is a loss of royal collectible look-alike spoons.

Yes, fear of loss works. Plus, the highest level of interest is now, not in some distant future when this infomercial is a blurred, forgotten memory. Now is better.

Fourth, testimonials. Humans love reviews and social proof. A video testimonial from another relatable human will help. Humans feel more secure in their decisions when others have made the same decision before them.

Will we want to be like an infomercial?

Probably not. But we can learn from infomercials.

When an infomercial producer spends tens of thousands of dollars in production, and then even more in paid advertising, we know there is something we can learn.

So let's enjoy late-night television infomercials. Entertaining, and a learning experience.

So what can we use to add value to our offers?

Could we add some free bonuses?

Prospects love something extra. If we sold protein shakes, it could be a free portable mixer so that they use our products more. If we sold skincare, we could add a unique portable makeup mirror.

And what about our business opportunity?

We could add coaching, a book on marketing, or even a report on tax tips for new businesses.

Do we have an interesting back story that builds confidence in our offer? This story could add extra value and confidence to our offers. Our prospects will think about this story often.

Could we offer a support community for our new customers and team members? This extra benefit alone could help prospects make their final decision.

It is important to remember that not every tactic used in infomercials will be appropriate for everyone. Let's think about our target audience and what will resonate with them. By using the right added-value tactics, we can create offers that are both valuable and persuasive.

SUMMARY

These 14 tools are great, but let's remember the big picture.

> #1. Find prospects who WANT what we offer.
> #2. Don't let our personal head trash sabotage our offer.
> #3. Create an offer … and then use the tools to improve our offer.

We don't have to use all these tools. The tools are to help us be more creative. The more options we have, the better our chances of creating an offer so powerful that most prospects will say "yes."

Great offers save time for us and our prospects. They decide if our offers work for them, or not. We save the details for those who want to take our offers.

And when we find that magical offer that works, we can pass on that offer to new team members. They can achieve immediate results while they learn the skills of network marketing.

Remember, one great offer can change our careers!

Let's start creating that offer now.

—Keith & Tom "Big Al" Schreiter

ABOUT THE AUTHORS

Keith Schreiter has 30+ years of experience in network marketing and MLM. He shows network marketers how to use simple systems to build a stable and growing business.

So, do you need more prospects? Do you need your prospects to commit instead of stalling? Want to know how to engage and keep your group active? If these are the types of skills you would like to master, you will enjoy his "how-to" style.

Keith speaks and trains in the U.S., Canada, and Europe.

Tom "Big Al" Schreiter has 50+ years of experience in network marketing and MLM. As the author of the original "Big Al" training books in the late '70s, he has continued to speak in over 80 countries on using the exact words and phrases to get prospects to open up their minds and say "YES."

His passion is marketing ideas, marketing campaigns, and how to speak to the subconscious mind in simplified, practical ways. He is always looking for case studies of incredible marketing campaigns that give usable lessons.

As the author of numerous audio trainings, Tom is a favorite speaker at company conventions and regional events.

MORE FROM
BIG AL BOOKS

See them all at BigAlBooks.com

Mindset Series

Secrets to Mastering Your Mindset
Take Control of Your Network Marketing Career

Breaking the Brain Code
Easy Lessons for Your Network Marketing Career

How to Get Motivated in 60 Seconds
The Secrets to Instant Action

Prospecting and Recruiting Series

The Happy Network Marketer
The Wealthy & Fun Way to Build My Business

Overcoming Objections
Making Network Marketing Rejection-Free

Hooks! The Invisible Sales Superpower
Create Network Marketing Prospects Who Want to Know More

How to Get Appointments Without Rejection
Fill Our Calendars with Network Marketing Prospects

Create Influence
10 Ways to Impress and Guide Others

How to Meet New People Guidebook
Overcome Fear and Connect Now

How to Get Your Prospect's Attention and Keep It!
Magic Phrases for Network Marketing

10 Shortcuts Into Our Prospects' Minds
Get Network Marketing Decisions Fast!

How To Prospect, Sell And Build Your Network Marketing Business With Stories

26 Instant Marketing Ideas To Build Your Network Marketing Business

51 Ways and Places to Sponsor New Distributors
Discover Hot Prospects For Your Network Marketing Business

First Sentences for Network Marketing
How To Quickly Get Prospects On Your Side

Big Al's MLM Sponsoring Magic
How To Build A Network Marketing Team Quickly

Start SuperNetworking!
5 Simple Steps to Creating Your Own Personal Networking Group

Getting Started Series

How to Build Your Network Marketing Business in 15 Minutes a Day

3 Easy Habits For Network Marketing
Automate Your MLM Success

Quick Start Guide for Network Marketing
Get Started FAST, Rejection-FREE!

Four Core Skills Series

How To Get Instant Trust, Belief, Influence and Rapport!
13 Ways To Create Open Minds By Talking To The Subconscious Mind

Ice Breakers!
How To Get Any Prospect To Beg You For A Presentation

Pre-Closing for Network Marketing
"Yes" Decisions Before The Presentation

The Two-Minute Story for Network Marketing
Create the Big-Picture Story That Sticks!

Personality Training Series (The Colors)

The Four Color Personalities for MLM
The Secret Language for Network Marketing

Mini-Scripts for the Four Color Personalities
How to Talk to our Network Marketing Prospects

Why Are My Goals Not Working?
Color Personalities for Network Marketing Success

How To Get Kids To Say Yes!
Using the Secret Four Color Languages to Get Kids to Listen

Presentation and Closing Series

Closing for Network Marketing
Getting Prospects Across The Finish Line

The One-Minute Presentation
Explain Your Network Marketing Business Like A Pro

How to Follow Up With Your Network Marketing Prospects
Turn Not Now Into Right Now!

Retail Sales for Network Marketers
How to Get New Customers for Your MLM Business

Leadership Series

The Complete Three-Book Network Marketing Leadership Series
Series includes: How To Build Network Marketing Leaders Volume One, How To Build Network Marketing Leaders Volume Two, and Motivation. Action. Results.

How To Build Network Marketing Leaders
Volume One: Step-By-Step Creation Of MLM Professionals

How To Build Network Marketing Leaders
Volume Two: Activities And Lessons For MLM Leaders

Motivation. Action. Results.
How Network Marketing Leaders Move Their Teams

What Smart Sponsors Do
Supercharge Our Network Marketing Team

More books...

Why You Need to Start Network Marketing
How to Remove Risk and Have a Better Life

How To Build Your Network Marketing Nutrition Business Fast

How Speakers, Trainers, and Coaches Get More Bookings
12 Ways to Flood Our Calendars with Paid Events

How To Build Your Network Marketing Utilities Business Fast

Getting "Yes" Decisions
What insurance agents and financial advisors can say to clients

Public Speaking Magic
Success and Confidence in the First 20 Seconds

Worthless Sponsor Jokes
Network Marketing Humor

.

Printed in Great Britain
by Amazon

26883075R00106